Yielding The New Life of God

Memories

by

Sister Claudette Marie Muhammad

God Is Love,

Sister Claudette
Marie
Muhammad

Foreword by
The Honorable Minister Louis Farrakhan

Publisher: FCI
Layout/Design: Harold Muhammad
Cover Photo: Leon Gurley
Inside Cover Photo: Ruth Muhammad
Photo Credits: Kenneth Muhammad, Monica Morgan and from author's
collection

Printed in the United States of America
ISBN -13: 978-1-929594-98-6
ISBN-10: 1-929594-98-4

Library of Congress Cataloging-in-Publication Data
Muhammad, Claudette Marie

Memories

is Written in Dedication of

My Beloved Mother, Ernestine Edith Johnson Mitchell

Who left us in 1975

and

My Dear Sister, Margurite Ann Johnson-Wilkins

who left us in 1970.

Memories

Dr. Margaret T. Burroughs, Senior Editor
Ms. Lori J. Taylor, First Editor

CONTENTS

Memories

Appendix

Foreword
By
The Honorable Minister Louis Farrakhan

I have been acquainted with Sister Claudette Marie Muhammad for a little over 20 years and she has worked with and for me for approximately 20 years. When you work closely with a person for many days, months and years under varied circumstances you begin to think that you know the person and you may think that you know the person quite well, but how many of us really know the persons that we take close to us or persons with whom we work? How many of us really get to know the persons with whom we interact on a daily basis? When Sister Claudette wrote this book, **"Memories"** and shared her life with me through this book, I realized how much I did not know about the person who has been working so closely with me for these many years. I have always respected Sister Claudette, her talents, her abilities and her zeal in getting a job done, but to know what makes a person who they are and what they are, you have to become acquainted with the things of their life that maybe you never speak of that helped to shape that person to be the person whom you ultimately meet.

After reading, **"Memories"**, I respected her more, I loved her more, because through this book I got to know the trials of her life and the ups and downs of her life that helped to shape the person that I met a little over 20 years ago. Her book, **"Memories"** made me to know how important it is for our children to know what their parents go through to get the children to where they are in life and her book made me to know that if parents shared with their children those things in life that shape them, the struggles that they went through, the victories and defeats of life, then we would never look outside of our homes for a hero, for, we would find in our moms, our dads and those who struggle to make a way for us, a true hero indeed.

Lastly, through my reading of her story in **"Memories,"** I realized more so that every human being is a book and that we would never get to know one another as fully as we could or should until our history is written and the nuances of our lives are brought forth, then and only then can people know who they truly walked with and among.

May Allah (God) bless Sister Claudette Marie Muhammad that her latter days will be better than her former days as she continues to write her testament of her history.

Louis Farrakhan

The Honorable Minister Louis Farrakhan

Preface

The following chapters are written as a collection of "memories" on many experiences I have had over the past sixty-nine years of my life. I was inspired to write "Memories" as a result of a meeting I had with the Honorable Minister Louis Farrakhan. In our meeting, he shared with me a few problems we had in securing first-class accommodations at a New York City hotel. I reminded him that as a former Vice-President of a travel agency, I knew what had transpired was inappropriate, not in accord with the standard hotel hospitality procedures with which I had become familiar. Upon completion of my noting the improprieties, The Minister sat back and in a quiet tone said to me, "Sister, you have done much, had many experiences and seem to know a great deal of people. We must one day sit down and talk of your experiences." I was touched by his words. Later, when I reflected on our conversation, the floodgates of my mind opened as vivid memories came as waves traced to my pen as I began to write "Memories". I was overwhelmed remembering so many experiences that were allowed by God. Love of family, close friendships, the people I've met, the places I've traveled, and the work I've done have been challenging, exhilarating, enlightening, passionate, motivating, sometimes on the edge, painful and even horrific. All of which have molded and shaped my life making me the person I am today. All experiences in one's life are, indeed, a teaching tool, a learning device to help one get to the next step in life. I have climbed many ladders, yet I am not tired because I truly believe God is not through with me. No, not yet.

God Is Love

Acknowledgments

For the many persons who read the draft manuscript of MEMORIES and who gave me words of encouragement towards getting MEMORIES published, I express my gratitude. There are so many persons that have inspired me, who have taught me, and who have guided me. Their knowledge, their grace, and skill have helped me to give birth to MEMORIES for which I am thankful.

First and foremost, I thank Almighty God Allah, who reminds me in Surah 2, Ayat 195: And Spend of your substance In the Cause of Allah, and make not your own hands contribute to (your destruction); But do good; For God loveth those Who do good. I thank my Minister, The Honorable Minister Louis Farrakhan for being the teacher that he is. Both my mother and father have gone on to Glory. I thank them for giving me life, and for each of my siblings who have allowed me to be "big sis". I am thankful to God for allowing me to be a Mother, Grandmother, and a Great-Grandmother, for my Godchildren and Spiritual Sons and Daughters.

For the many friends and associates (there are too many to list) I thank you for lending an ear, for a whisper of encouragement and support. For the men who have come and gone in my life allowing me the experience of romantic love, even though the relationships ended, I thank you because you gave me the insight of sharing and the experience of feeling the pain of sorrow as the relationship ended. Yet, and probably more importantly, I've grown to know that nothing happens without reason.

In all, I am a better person today because of everyone who has touched my life and, prayerfully, their touch will help to make me better for what I will become tomorrow.

To God Be The Glory

Memories

In the Beginning

In 1938 on a Sunday, the morning of February 13th, at Jefferson Davis Hospital, in Houston, Texas, Ernestine Edith Henderson-Johnson, gave birth to her first child, Claudette Marie Johnson. My father, Travis Johnson II, was overjoyed. He was not disappointed by not having a boy, for he knew that God would bless him with many more children, both boys and girls. Within the following eighteen years, God did just that, for my dad became the father of fifteen children (eight boys and seven girls), one boy died at birth and one daughter, his second child, was brutally murdered at the age of thirty-one.

I was the apple of my father's eye. He took me everywhere with him, the pool-hall, riding in his truck as he made errands (making extra money to support his growing family), to church on Sundays, visiting relatives, and when he would go fishing. My mother was giving birth year after year, and as I began to come into my young years, I helped her with my brothers and sisters. I learned to clean house, to separate the colored clothes from the white clothes (sometimes saying to myself, this was like the Black folk and the White folk), run the hot water and soak the clothes for washing. I would get a chair at the age of four and a half, stand at the stove and pour cream-of-wheat and/or oatmeal in a pot of boiling water, stir it until it thickened, take the pot off the stove and prepare breakfast for my siblings, with a hot biscuit or toast, and a glass of whole milk.

At the age of five, I realized my father had joined the Navy. My mother taught me about the war. It was called World War II. I saw pictures and would hear stories that my mother would read to me. My dad would write letters from overseas. My mother would steam off the stamps and read what my father had written on the back of the stamps, because my mother told me that the officers would oft-times read the enlisted men's mail. They didn't want certain things to be sent in writing back to the families of the sailors.

Little Girl, Big Secret

My paternal grandfather, Travis Johnson Sr., would often come to visit us. Sometimes he spent the night. I would never really get close to him, because I often felt strange around him. He and his sister were offspring of a White father and a mother who was half American Choctaw Indian and Negro. He smoked a pipe and the smell would make me feel sick. One evening he came to our house, ate dinner that my mother had prepared, played with us, and went into our bedroom to go to bed. He put me in the bed with him. Early the next morning, I woke up with Papa Travis on top of me. He had gone inside of me, tearing my vagina, splitting it to my rectum. Although, I tried to be silent, I knew that my grandfather was doing something very wrong to me. It reached the point where the pain and the smell of my grandfather were so overbearing, I screamed. My mother was in the kitchen cooking breakfast. She heard me scream, picked up a broom, ran into the bedroom and beat her father-in-law with the broom. He jumped up off me, picked up his clothes and ran out of the house. My mother picked me up, yelled at the children to stay in the house, and ran with me in her arms to her mother-in-law's home. At the house stayed her mother-in-law's mother who was half Blackfoot Indian and Black. She had left her reservation some years ago to stay with her daughter because she was up in age. They put me in my great-grandmother's room. She laid me on a blanket on the floor, took sage and other herbs and soaked me where I had been so savagely damaged, burned incense and chanted Indian prayers. For two weeks, I went in and out of consciousness. I had a burning fever because infection had set in.

Sarah Johnson, my paternal grandmother begged my mother not to tell my father, what had happened. She said if you do, he will kill his father. My mother cried and cried. She was so saddened that this had happened to me. I heard my grandmother tell my mother that oft-times she would sleep in the room with her own daughters to keep her husband from sexually abusing them.

Neither Travis, who she called Brother, nor his two brothers knew this about their father. Sarah had six children, three boys and three girls. After two weeks, I finally healed physically, but mentally, I knew that to trust a man or allow a man to get close to me would be difficult. The secret stayed within the family. My mother never told my father, and I never told him. He passed some eighty plus years later, never knowing what his father had done to his first born child.

My mother was close to her mother, Margurite Rixner-Henderson Hall. Her mother's mother was a Creole woman, whose name was Ernestine Cardova. She was Black, French and Russian, and her father Portuguese, Negro, and American Cherokee Indian. They were from New Orleans, Louisiana, and spoke a Creolized language. My mother did not know much about her birth father. She was close to his sister and his sister's daughter. They were from Hearne, Texas. Ernestine's mother married Mr. Hall, a very stern man who was a railroad Pullman Porter. The Pullman Porters were the workers on the railroad trains. They took care of the passengers on the sleeping and dining cars. The Pullman Porters were instrumental in the success of the passenger railroad industry. When the Pullman Company first started, they hired in the beginning, only Blacks. A. Philip Randolph was the President of the Pullman Porters. He was instrumental in many changes in politics, as it related to Black folk. He worked closely with Reverend Dr. Martin Luther King. My grandfather and great uncle, Richard Cebrun were both Railroad Pullman Porters. Ernestine's mother's sister, Belle Cebrun, was a community activist. To this day, a street (Cebrun) is named after her on the corner of Paul Quinn and Cebrun, where her home remains in Houston, Texas.

After I was healed, my mother moved near her aunt's home, and later moved in with her aunt, who owned acres of land. Behind her home, she owned and operated a café. I worked at a very early age in my aunt's café. Me, my aunt and my aunt's husband, Richard Cebrun, were very close. My grandmother's brother, Eugene Rixner and his wife Sadie, who was a Creole of Black, Indian, Chinese and White heritage, lived next door. He was a "Buffalo Soldier." They would tell me stories about Black history, and the lifestyle of their parents' when they lived in Louisiana. The stories helped me in my youth to begin to understand the plight of my people.

Old Faces- New Spaces

After my father came home from the war, he seemed somewhat changed. I would often hear him and my mother argue. I was grown far beyond my years. I would sit and listen to the adults talk. In my aunt's café, I would listen to the men and women who often had meetings to discuss the racial problems within their community. My aunt would go to City Hall meetings and discuss the living conditions of her people. She was active in the church. Me and my siblings went to church from sunrise 'til sundown. We knew Sister so-and-so and Brother so-and-so. I would help the Pastor and his wife in the church. I knew much of the Church's business.

My grandmother, Margurite and her husband, moved to California. When things became bitter between my mother and father, my mother packed up some of her children, and moved to San Diego, California to be with her mother and stepfather. We traveled by train and thanks to my uncle and grandfather, who worked the railroad, we were well taken care of on that train journey from Houston, Texas to San Diego, California. She left behind one daughter and two of her sons. The one daughter followed within the year, but my dad kept the two boys, who did not come and live with us until they were in their teens.

Upon graduating from Junior High School, I was presented with a gift from my Aunt Cebrun, a roundtrip ticket to visit Houston, Texas. I was fifteen years of age at the time. I spent the summer with my aunt and uncle. I visited my father, who would often write to me asking that I give his love to my mother and sisters, yet he never sent a penny to help my mother financially. He remarried and had at that time, three boys by his present wife, Ray Johnson. Their first born son, died at child birth. He and Ray later had two girls and one son. The son was born one year prior to the birth of my son, Anthony La Mare.

While in Houston, spending the summer with family, I visited all of my relatives. I talked to everyone about my family, learning the family history. One day, while visiting my father's sister, in walks Papa Travis. One look at him and I recalled what he had done to me some ten and a half years earlier. There I was facing my grandfather, with my father, his sister and my cousins looking at the two of us. As my grandfather approached me saying, "come on honey give your grandpa a kiss," with others looking on, I hugged him and said in a very low voice "satan get behind me, God knows what you did, and you will pay." My grandfather stood back, turned red and began to cough. My father and aunt said, "dad what's wrong? Are you ill?" He said, "I'm alright, I feel extremely hot." He left and I never saw or heard about him until many years later, when one of my father's daughters called to say he had passed. I said "thank you for calling. I pray he burns in hell." Until this day, I don't know if my sister who called, told our father or any family member what I had said.

After that summer, I returned back to San Diego. I excelled in High School. I became a "Junior Achiever", a program that involved me in various aspects in Community Relations for the youth. I was a Junior Representative of the N.A.A.C.P. and the Urban League, going as a youth delegate to the Convention of The Urban League and N.A.A.C.P. I was selected to be "introduced" to society by a national organization that sponsored a "Black and White" Debutante Ball. All the young girls had to wear a white formal gown. Being that this was also my senior year, I had to also have a gown for my senior prom. My mother managed somehow to get both gowns. One of her military friends in his full formal military attire, escorted my mother and I to the Debutante Ball. There I was along with twelve other young women being "introduced" to society. All of us who participated were carefully selected on merits of our academic standing and community participation.

Beauty Has No Race

After graduating from high school, I became actively involved in politics. I was a member of the Young Democrats. I also took up modeling, enrolling in John Robert Powers School of Modeling, one of the most prestigious modeling schools in the country. Many of the models went to a certain beauty salon in San Diego to get their hair done, especially prior to a modeling assignment. I made an appointment. I noticed that for hours I sat and no one came to assist me. Finally, I asked for the manager and he told me, "We don't do colored people's hair." Here it was in the mid-1950's, I had never actually faced racism to know it, and was now being slapped in the face with racism. I got their business card, confirmed that I actually had a reservation, and took the manager's name. I then went to the President of the N.A.A.C.P., who took me to an attorney. A law suit was filed. During the court hearing, the Judge said, "My wife is Hungarian, she has soft-like hair, hard to manage. I would hate to even think that if she went to that beauty salon, she would be turned down because of the texture of her hair." After I took the witness stand, and my lawyer finished with the owner of that beauty salon, the Judge favored me. I won my civil law suit. It was in the headlines of The San Diego Tribune, the neighborhood local press, and radio news, "Claudette Won!" I continued my course at the modeling school, and sent many of my Black girlfriends to that beauty salon, who had by then hired a Black beautician to take care of their Black clients.

I entered San Diego Junior College. I worked as a librarian where I had worked for the City Libraries since the 10th grade. A few months later, I was asked to enter "Miss Bronze California." I did and made 2nd runner-up to the winner. Some years later in Chicago, while working in the Nation of Islam, I was acquainted with Dr. Donald Torry, who had married the winner a year after the Miss Bronze contest. I continued with my studies at San Diego Junior College. In a relationship that was not in my favor, I became pregnant and gave birth to my son, Anthony La Mare, just five days prior to my twenty-first birthday.

Trusted and Betrayed

I was twenty when I met James S. Robinson, and was deeply involved with Braxton Pinkins, a famous College basketball and football player, who was contracted to go on and play professional basketball. He was popular with the ladies. We dated. Some months later, he asked my mother and stepfather (my mother had remarried after all those years of being a single mom) for my hand in marriage. He promised them that after he graduated, he would go on to play professional basketball and would take good care of me. We announced our engagement party that was to be held at my mother's home the next two weeks. A week prior to my engagement party, I was on a modeling assignment for a benefit show. In the audience were many of my friends. After the show, I was introduced to a young handsome brother who was in the Marine Corps. We talked and talked. He was from my birth city of Houston, Texas. He called me the next day and invited me to lunch. Jimmy, as he was called, was a bit older then I, both in years and street life. I tried to be all grown-up. At lunch, we ordered drinks, had wine with dinner and after we ate, had drinks after dinner. By now my head was spinning. I had never smoked or drank. Being that I was quite tipsy, I couldn't go home and let my family see me in that condition. Jimmy offered for me to go and rest at his friend's home. He said in a few hours I would be alright. We went to his friend's home. I was so out of it, I could hardly keep myself together. I laid down, fell asleep, and later when I woke up, Jimmy was next to me. Well, we know what happened. I hurried and dressed and told him to get me home. It was around eleven at night. I never stayed out past mid-night, for I was living in my mother's home and would not want her to be concerned about me. Whenever I was out, she would stay up until I got home.

I didn't see Jimmy anymore in terms of dating. Braxton and I had our engagement party. Jimmy and many of my friends and Braxton's friends attended. We had a grand time. I was officially engaged, beautiful engagement ring, and well on my way to getting married. The following month I missed my monthly cycle, but that was not unusual because I often missed, but never thought of being pregnant because I was not doing anything that would get me pregnant. Braxton and I, after becoming formally engaged, did become intimate. My thought was, well we are going to get married, so it was alright. Once I learned that I was indeed pregnant, I said to Braxton, let's move our wedding date up. He became nervous and would not give me an answer. I finally learned from his sister-in-law that he was not legally divorced. I felt like a ton of bricks had hit me. I approached him and he acknowledged that, yes, he was not legally divorced. He had a wife and children back in Indiana. I was furious. We actually fought. The engagement was off. Here I was pregnant, with no husband. What a disgrace to bring on my family. I didn't want to be at home with my younger sisters who would have to see me in that condition, and when their friends came to our home there might be embarrassment for them. To prevent that, I moved in with my sister who had recently gotten a divorce. I took care of her two children while she worked and went to nursing school. I moved back to my mother's home, just prior to giving birth to my son.

After my son was born, Braxton and I went to court. He had a friend who had been in college with him. They both had been on the basketball team together. He was now an Assistant District Attorney. I was ordered by the court for me and my son to take a blood test. The test came back with results reporting that Braxton was not the father. My mother, Braxton, his friend the Assistant D.A. and I, all held a meeting. I was questioned about the situation of my pregnancy. My mother and I both thought there had been some foul play with the D.A. showing favoritism to Braxton. All of a sudden I heard my mother begin to curse. I had never in my life heard her use a curse word. Well, she cursed out Braxton and the Assistant D.A., grabbed me up out of my chair, and told both of them to go to hell. She said, "my daughter don't need a damn thing from either of you. God will take care of she and her son." We stormed out of the office. I never looked back. God has done just what my mother said. He has taken

11

good care of my son and I. Blessed us in so many ways. In all the years of raising my son, I never wanted for anything.

Being that the blood test demonstrated that Braxton was not the father of my child, I couldn't believe he was not, because I had not been involved with anyone else, with the exception of that one night with Jimmy. I wrote him a letter. He by now was out of the Marines and was back in Houston, Texas. He called me after getting my letter and suggested I come to Houston, Texas, and maybe we would get married. I didn't take him seriously. If he wanted me, I felt he should have come for me. He never would admit that he was the father of my child. Our paths crossed many times. When I was modeling with Ebony Fashion Fair, and a couple of times when he came to D.C. He called and once he saw Tony, but he would never own up to the fact that he, not Braxton had fathered my child. Some twenty-plus years, while I was working with Minister Farrakhan, he called to ask me about the Minister. He said that Imam W. Deen Mohammad had hired him to do some legal work. I received his call, and told him the Minister would soon be in Houston, Texas for a speaking engagement. I invited him to come. He did and we seated him in the V.I.P. section. My family, including my dad was there so I didn't have the time to introduce Jimmy to the Minister. That was in 1984. I saw him once more when Minister Farrakhan was speaking in D.C., staying at the Howard Inn, there Jimmy was in the lobby. He and a White woman, whom I was told, they later married. To my knowledge, that was his second wife. He divorced her and married again. Until a few years ago, I never shared the knowledge with my son of his birth father, nor any member of my family. Sometimes its best to keep things locked in one's heart. I am the elder of all my brother and sisters. I have never wanted them, my son, my mother nor grandmother to be pained because of any problems I may have had in my life.

When I shared this with my son, only a few years ago, I told him that he could get a court order, have a DNA test, and learn the truth about his biological father. He said, "The hell with that, I'm fine. He has not attempted to be with me all these years, I don't need him now."

Back on my feet, I moved from my mother's home into my own apartment. I didn't want to work because I felt it was important to be with my son during his first year of development. I secured welfare assistance for eleven months. The social worker would from time to time come to my apartment for inspections. I kept a clean apartment, my son clean and well dressed, and kept his health record for the social worker to review.

On one visit, a social worker (there would be different social workers), came to my apartment. She noticed how clean my apartment was. In the bedroom she looked at the curtains and bedspread, and said to me, "The curtains and bedspread are beautiful. They look expensive." I told her yes, they were expensive, because I had purchased expensive material and hand- made the curtains and bedspread. Sewing had been taught to me by both my mother and grandmother. The social worker then told me, "You keep such a clean house, can do beautiful handcraft, and I'm sure you can cook well, why don't you get married?" Why did she say that? My Indian blood began to boil. I said to that White social worker, "I'm sure you keep a clean house. I don't know what skills you have in homemaking. Are you married?" The social worker said she was not married. I said to her, "Why don't you get married?" I went on to say to the social worker, that it was not her job to come and insult me. Whether I was married or not, was none of her business. I told the social worker that this was not the South and that she as a White woman, could not come into a Black woman's home and insult her. The social worker saw how she had angered me, and began to quickly make her exit. I shortly thereafter stop receiving public assistance, got a job as a Technical Librarian with General Dynamics/ Astronautics, working with scientific and technical writers, who wrote manuals for the structure of the Atlas and Centur Missiles. The first missile was launched in the early 1960's at Vandenberg Air Force Base in California.

I was, by now, enjoying motherhood, loving the moments I had with my son, and relaxing much with my family. My brother and his wife had moved in the apartment complex where I was living. We oft-times had great family gatherings.

A friend introduced me to a handsome, good-looking military man, Ralph Palmer, who seemed to take an interest in my son and me. We began to date, and later became engaged. Then one day, I discovered what I had experienced just a few years ago, I was pregnant again. I was happy because here I was engaged to, what I thought, was a beautiful brother. All we had to do was get married. Well, he hit the ceiling when he learned I was pregnant. He took me to one of his friends. An older woman who seemed to be quite worldly. The woman told me that Ralph wanted her to take me across the border of San Diego to Mexico and get an abortion. I was frightened as could be. I didn't share with my mother nor any family member of my situation other than one of my sisters. Being that Ralph didn't want to rush into marriage, nor did he want me to have his child, and I was not going to have a second child out of wedlock, I allowed the woman to take me to Mexico. I had the abortion of a male child, stayed with the doctor and his family for two days, and returned across the border by myself on a bus. It was a horrible experience. I never told my mother, grandmother nor any of my siblings. The sister who knew I was pregnant, thought I had a miscarriage. I became quite ill, as a result of the abortion, and had to go into the hospital for surgery, which was the beginning, throughout the years, of six major operations and finally at the young age of thirty-three, I had to have a hysterectomy.

After I got out of the hospital from my first surgery, I went, with my son, to have a full one-on-one meeting with my priest. He heard my confession, and afterwards took me and my son, to his study and blessed us both. He told me never to look back on what I had done. God through His son, Jesus The Christ, had forgiven me. He told me that the gates of heaven would open and God would flood me with many Blessings. At the end of our session, he reminded me that life is a trial. If we fail in one aspect of our lives, God would open the door so that we could pass through, and grasp on to another aspect, keeping our hand in God's Hand we would not go wrong. He reminded me that life is full of lessons. He told me to learn the lessons well and take life's journey in peace.

That Priest and I remained in contact throughout the years. When I was chosen by Congressman Van Deerlin, who was elected in 1963 as the Democratic Congressman from the 37th District in my home city of San Diego, California, to go to Washington, D.C., the Priest said, "see, God has opened another door for you, walk through it and never look back."

Some twenty years later, I received a call at my D.C. residence. It was Ralph Palmer. He called to say, "I'm sorry for the way I treated you." I accepted his apology and hung up the phone. I have never heard from him again.

Football and Modeling

When my son was about two years of age, my mother and her husband asked for my son and I to move in with them. There were now only two girls at home, as all the others had married and moved into their own homes. Living next door was Ernie Barnes, one of the San Diego Chargers football players. He and his family became friendly with my family. He asked me if I would tryout for the "Chargettes," a cheering team of girls who danced at halftime at the San Diego Chargers Football games, also visited hospital clinics and schools, representing the football team. He told my mother that there were all White girls in the Chargettes, no Blacks and that the Black football players had gotten together to have the owners select a Black girl. He told me and my mother that he and Ernie Ladd, Earl Faison, Ernie Wright and a few other Black players had given the owners my name. Several of the Black players' wives went with me for the tryouts, and as God Willed it, I won in the tryouts. We performed at all the games, did TV commercials, and I was one of the spokespersons. I became quite active in representing the San Diego Chargers football team. I was the first Black girl who performed at half-time of any football game of the American Football League.

I was asked by one of the White workers at General Dynamics, to look at a <u>Life Magazine</u>. There was a Negro photographer who had published a beautiful photograph of his wife and other Black women in the magazine. She said to me, you should meet the photographer, his name is Gordon Parks. He was showing the beauty of Black women. She told me that I should go out and model, because I was as beautiful as these Black women in the magazine. I had my child to support. I was active in the Young Democrats and other civic organizations. I could not chase after a modeling career, not knowing if I would get a weekly paycheck. I had responsibilities.

General Dynamics / Astronautics

My supervisor came and asked me if I would be willing to travel to a military off-site base housed in Omaha, Nebraska to work with the Scientific and Technical Writers. He told me not only would I receive my weekly salary, but seventy-five dollars a day per diem to cover my daily expenses (hotel, travel, and food). After discussing this with my mother and stepfather, I left my son in their care, and trekked off to Omaha, Nebraska. Prior to my travel, I had arranged with the President of the Urban League to find me a family to live with, and had gotten in touch with one of the men who would be working at the Air Force Base, to pick me up, to and from work, which meant I could save that seventy-five dollars a day per-diem. The family the Urban League had chosen for me to stay with did not charge me any rent, and the man who drove me to and from the job did not charge me any money. I learned a lot while working in Omaha, Nebraska. The team of Scientific and Technical Writers were made up of "Whites," one "Indian," two "Mexicans," and one "Black" (me). The Blacks in Omaha who knew of my assignment with working on the structural design of the missile, were quite proud of me. I had speaking engagements at the N.A.A.C.P. meetings, the Urban League and several of the Women's sororities. I met wonderful folk all of whom took me in like family.

After the project was finished, one of my Mexican colleagues and I, drove back to San Diego from Omaha, Nebraska, stopping off in New Mexico and Houston, Texas, where we visited with my family. The Mexican co-worker who drove with me, said members of my family looked like some of the Mexicans in her family.

A Whirlwind of Worth

After returning to San Diego, I became quite active in the Chollas Democratic Club. It was one of the largest Democratic Clubs in San Diego that had a majority of "Blacks." I became the secretary of the Democratic Club. A news journalist who was an anchor on one of the San Diego T.V. stations, decided to run for the 37th Congressional District. In his platform, one of the things he said, "Once elected, I will do what no other Congressman has done from San Diego. I will hire a Black secretary and take her to Washington, D.C." That of course, along with Lionel Van Deerlin's political issues got the "Black vote". He kept his word. Out of fifty young Black women who applied for the position, I was chosen with the support of the Chollas Democratic Club.

The headline of the December 13, 1962, Volume 11, No. 61, *The Voice*, a San Diego newspaper, read:

"Claudette Johnson Named to Post with Van Deerlin"

"In a precedent-setting appointment, beautiful and brainy Miss Claudette Marie Johnson, daughter of Mr. and Mrs. Frazier Mitchell of 5510 Dream Street, will step into the post of secretary to Congressman-Elect Lionel Van Deerlin.

Miss Johnson will work from Mr. Van Deerlin's Washington, D.C. Congressional Offices and will officially assume her position on January 3rd, 1963. She will leave San Diego on December 27th.

Miss Johnson's appointment comes as a Direct result of the Chollas Democratic Club's Insistence upon minority job opportunities in Politics. Chollas Club's Executive Board selected Miss Johnson and passed the recommendation on to Mr. Van Deerlin last Friday evening. Mr. Van Deerlin acted upon it immediately.

Miss Johnson is presently employed as a librarian at General Dynamics Astronautics Company, where she has served for the past year.

From September, 1961 to February, 1962, Miss
Johnson traveled for the company to military off-site
Bases on a research program.

Brought to San Diego at the age of seven,
Miss Johnson has attended Stockton and Sherman
Elementary Schools in San Diego; Dana Junior High
School and Point Loma High School in Point Loma;
And graduated from Kearny High School. She ma-
jored in Business Administration at San Diego Junior
College and in Elementary Education at San Diego
State College.

The newly appointed secretary has served as
secretary to the Chollas Democratic Club, is a member
of the Membership Committee of the NAACP, and a
member of the San Diego Chargettes."

In December of 1962, I took a train from San Diego, California to Chicago, Illinois, where I visited my close friend, Floyd
Robinson who was from San Diego. He played baseball with the
Chicago White Sox. I spent a week with him. He introduced me
to Jerri Spencer, wife of one of the "Step Brothers." We became
friends, and when I returned a year later to Chicago, modeling
with Ebony Fashion Fair, Jerri Spencer took charge introducing
me to Chicago's "Black Society".

Floyd Robinson put me on a plane to Washington, D.C. He
didn't want me riding the train. He told me that I would be traveling through cities and he didn't feel comfortable because all
kinds of people took the train. He purchased a plane ticket and
sent me on my way. Washington, D.C., what a city! Sterling
Tucker, President of the D.C. Chapter of the Urban League, had
gotten a call from the San Diego Chapter President, asking him
to look after me once I arrived in D.C. I got myself a room at the
Y.W.C.A., and later moved in with a family Sterling Tucker had
found for me to stay.

One evening, Sterling Tucker invited me for dinner. At
dinner was Whitney Young. They talked and talked. I was not
aware who Whitney Young was, until toward the end of our dinner. Mr. Young asked me, "You don't know who I am, do you?"
I said, "No, I don't, other than you are a friend of Sterling Tucker." Sterling Tucker and Whitney Young laughed. I was then

told by Mr. Young that he was the recently appointed National Director of the Urban League. I felt quite embarrassed. As much volunteer work I had previously done with the Urban League and given how much the President of the San Diego and Omaha, Nebraska Chapters, as well as Sterling Tucker in D.C. had helped me, I didn't know that Whitney Young was the National President. He told me that he was quite impressed by the conversation we had shared at dinner, and that he thought I was well versed on present day issues, with not only Blacks, but with the politics of the world. He offered me a job at their National Headquarters. I thanked him and said that I was happy in my present position with Congressman Van Deerlin. Some twenty-five years later, while in Chicago working with the Honorable Minister Louis Farrakhan, I met a very wonderful woman, who was quite actively involved in community affairs, an educator and lover of the arts. She was Dr. Arnita Boswell, who during a conversation, we discussed our family background. Dr. Boswell told me that her brother (now deceased) was Whitney Young of the Urban League. I shared with Dr. Boswell that years ago, I had met and had dinner with her brother and Sterling Tucker, and that he had offered me a job in the Urban League's National Headquarters. Dr. Boswell laughed and said, "Yes, I bet he did. He loved beautiful, intelligent women." I thought, "What a small world".

Being that I was a former San Diego Chargette for the American League San Diego Chargers football team, I applied for a position with the Redskinettes of the Washington Redskins football team. Here, again, I experienced discrimination which was like a slap in my face. After being refused by management of the Washington Redskins, I went to the Washington, D.C. Urban League. The discrimination charge hit the 1964 edition of the *Washington Post*—"*Model's brown skin is nixed by the Redskins*":

> Miss Claudette Johnson's brown skin kept
> her from becoming a Redskinette, the pretty model
> and Congressional secretary charged.
> **After Miss Johnson was turned down, Sterling**

Tucker, executive director of the Washington Urban
   League, wrote to Leo De Orsey, vice president of the
   Redskins, suggesting the Redskins include colored in
   the band, majorettes, cheerleaders and front office.

The letter was sent June 11 but so far, Tucker
has not received a reply.

MISS JOHNSON, who had a year's experience as
Chargette with the San Deigo Chargers football team
applied for a job as a Redskinette last year.

In response to a telephone inquiry, she received
a letter from the Redskins announcing the date of
the next tryouts.

She was one of girls who showed up, including
another colored applicant.

* * *

IN GROUPS of threes, the girls executed a dance
routine under the direction of an instructor and "strutted
around the room" to music.

About a week later, Miss Johnson received a
letter from the Redskins informing her that there were
no vacancies but should one occur, she would be informed
of future tryouts.

"If they hadn't needed Red-held skinettes, they
wouldn't have place," was her reaction.

* * *

MISS JOHNSON desegregated the San Diego
Chargettes in 1962 before coming to the District a year
later first to work for Congressman Lionel [Van] Deerlin.

Her interest in becoming a Redskinette is an out-
growth of a hobby, modeling. She was one of the Ebony
fashion models last year.

Redskinettes are hostesses at Redskins social
functions and perform a dance routine during game half-
times.

* * *

[NEITHER DE ORSEY nor board member Milton
King could be reached for comment on Tucker's letter.] De
Orsey was reportedly in Connecticut and King at the GOP
convention in San Francisco.

Edward Bennett Williams, famed criminal attorney,
   who is also a member of the board said Redskins board
   next week on overall problems involving the football
   team and presumably, Tucker's letter will be one of the matters discussed.

Chester Minter, administrative assistant to De Orsey,
declined to comment.

* * *

IN HIS LETTER, Tucker stated: "I know that
Redskins fans are appreciative of the continuing efforts
of management to build a first class organization in every way.

In this connection, it would seem timely and most
appropriate for the Redskins to include colored in its band,
majorette and the cheerleading groups, as well as in its front
office.

We believe that the football public will applaud such
progress, and the Washington Urban League is prepared to assist in the recruitment of qualified talent."

Capitol Hill Years

Congressman Van Deerlin told me that I was to work hard, learn what I could, and keep a moral character about myself. There were just a few Black Congressional Secretaries back in the early sixties. Congressman Adam Clayton Powell (D-NY), had met me. He took a liking to me, and would share with me the politics of the city. He introduced me to Corrine Huff, one of his secretaries, who was also his companion. I met Congressman Charles Diggs (D-MI), and several of the other Black Congressmen, namely Congressman Robert Nelson Nix (D-PA) and Congressman Gus Hawkins (D-CA). I also met Congressman Paul Findley (D-IL) a White Congressman who would invite me to his office. He recognized that I was part Indian. He represented Indians in his Congressional District. We would discuss the plight of my Indian brothers and sisters. I learned much from Congressman Findley. I would visit all their offices and have lengthy conversations with them, learning so much of the ends-and-outs on Capitol Hill.

In 1963, Maurice Sorrell, a photographer for Jet magazine, met me. He told me that I should become an Ebony Fashion Fair Model. I told him that Howard Morehead, a Jet magazine photographer in Los Angeles, California, a year ago had told me the same, and also one of my former White co-workers after showing me photos by Gordon Parks. I really didn't feel that secure in pursuing a modeling career. Maurice Sorrell got in touch with John H. Johnson, Publisher of Johnson Publications, also with Simeon Booker, Washington, D.C. Bureau Chief for Jet magazine. By this time, I was active in all kinds of activities in Washington, D.C.

I had moved again with another family, met many friends and was dating a dentist who had a host of friends. One person I met was Andrew Hatcher, who was the deputy press secretary to President Kennedy under his press secretary, Pierre Sallinger. Andrew Hatcher invited me to the White House, where he treated me to lunch in the Cabinet Members' dining room. Joining

us for lunch was Ethel Payne, a well established media personality. Mrs. Jackie Kennedy was also having lunch at the same
time, and Andrew Hatcher introduced me to her. She was a very
kind and genuine person. At lunch, Ethel Payne spoke at length,
sharing with me that, although, I was a beautiful young woman
moving in and out of the D.C. political and social circle, to be
careful and always keep a moral character about myself. Andrew
Hatcher listened as Ethel Payne spoke, and told me that was one
of the reasons he had invited me to lunch, was so that I could
hear a word from the wise. He told me that many young Negro
women had come to D.C. and some had fallen by the wayside
because of their immoral conduct. I thanked them both and Ethel
Payne's words have stayed with me 'til this day. Years later,
while working in the Nation of Islam, I arranged for Ethel Payne
to have lunch with The Honorable Minister Louis Farrakhan.
Ethel Payne later told me, "See how God has blessed you? To be
at the foot of such a great man is indeed a blessing."

Ebony Fashion Fair

I was chosen by the late John H. Johnson and his wife, Eunice, to become one of their 1963 models for the Ebony Fashion Fair. What an experience! I traveled to fifty-seven cities, meeting people from all walks of life. The tour was exciting. The models all traveled together on a tour bus. Arriving to a city in Oklahoma, as we were getting off the tour bus, going into our hotel, the bellman while taking me and my roommate's (Terri Springer) luggage to our room said, "Have you heard the good news? President Kennedy has been shot and killed." The "good news." I wanted to slap that White bellman. All I could do was get in my room and pray for the Kennedy family. I called Congressman Van Deerlin. He told me to be careful, and if I wanted to quit the tour I could come back to D.C. and continue working in his office. He had given me a four month leave of absence. I had gotten much recognition on the tour with the Ebony Fashion Fair Show; on the cover of <u>Jet</u> magazine, in another issue the centerfold of <u>Jet</u>, media coverage in the <u>Roll Call</u> (the newspaper on Capitol Hill), and in the <u>San Diego Tribune</u>. I "thanked" my Congressman and continued on the Tour, because I had signed up and given my word to John H. Johnson, and his wife Eunice, who was the Director of the Ebony Fashion Fair Tour. Not only that, I could not allow "fear" to prevent me from doing what I wanted to do.

I will always hold Mrs. Eunice and Mr. John H. Johnson dear to my heart. They both did so much for those of us who were their Ebony Fashion Fair Models. We received a tremendous education. Not only did we, as models, grace the runways in the major cities throughout the country, but we appeared on television and radio programs, speaking on our experiences as a Fashion Fair Model. We did so much in terms of Community Service and Commercials for various products. As Ebony Fashion Fair Models, we showed the world, beauty of the Black Woman. My experiences as a "Centerfold" model in <u>Jet</u> magazine and years later at the 25th Anniversary Celebration of Ebony Fashion Fair, held in New York, whereby one model from each year within those past twenty-five years, my being selected as the model from 1963, helped me to be the woman I am today. I'm truly grateful to Mr. and Mrs. John H. Johnson. Mr. Johnson instilled in us to always value our self-worth, keep high moral standards, and know that we are truly special. My experiences as an Ebony Fashion Fair Model have helped me in every facet of my life. After the tour, I spent time with my son and family in San Diego, California. I had become quite a celebrity. Many of the Blacks in my community looked at me as having accomplished success. I knew that God had a purpose in life for me, and that nothing or no one would set me back. The mistakes I had made were all a learning process for me to keep on keeping on.

A Monster

Eight months after I gave birth to my son, I drove to Los Angeles, California with friends. We were going to a Los Angeles Rams football game and were to return to San Diego the next day. We stopped at a friend's home. The friend and others went to the grocery store to purchase food, and they went to a clothing store to get new outfits for the game. I was extremely tired. I laid down on the couch to rest and fell asleep. I woke up to have a man on top of me. I later learned that he was the cousin of our host. He sexually abused me and had me in a choke hold, whereby I couldn't fight him off to protect myself. After he raped me, he went back into his room. Our host had not told me that her cousin was in one of the bedrooms asleep. If she had, I would have had reservations to stay there alone in the house. Once our host and friends that I had traveled with returned, and although I had tried to get myself together, our host sensed something was wrong. Our host took me aside and she questioned me. I broke down and told her what had happened. Neither I nor our host told the others. The cousin was a very popular person. He had a household name, nationwide. I thought, if I went to the police, who would believe me? A single parent not married and the man, being who he was, no one would believe me. I had to go on like nothing had happened. Until this day, I have never seen that person again, and do not know if he is alive or dead. The secret of the rape stayed with me and the cousin.

Exit Dallas

After visiting with my family in San Diego, at the end of the Ebony Fashion Fair Tour, I traveled back to Washington, D.C., stopping off in Dallas, Texas. I stayed at the Hilton Hotel. Myself and a friend went to the restaurant at the hotel. We had called and made reservations, giving my name and room number. We stood waiting to be seated. Whites were coming in, getting seated, but yet me and my friend were overlooked. Finally, I asked for the manager. I let him know that reservations had been made, that I was a guest at the hotel, and why was it that my friend and I were being mistreated. The manager told me "We don't serve colored folk. You can order food and eat in your hotel room." I was furious. I went to the front desk manager and demanded an apology. He told me that Negroes were not served in their restaurant. I told him that the N.A.A.C.P., the Urban League, and the Press would hear about this. The manager told me not to start trouble. He said they would send me and my friend a free meal to my room. I went to my room and called Congressman Van Deerlin. He told me to pack my bags and get the first flight out of Dallas. He reminded me that President Kennedy, just three months earlier, had been killed in that very same city. Congressman Van Deerlin then called the manager of the hotel, and said to him that I was his personal secretary, that no harm should come to me. He told the manager that I would leave the hotel the next morning. Needless to say, I did as the Congressman instructed, but I wanted to inform the N.A.A.C.P. and the Urban League. I left Dallas quite upset, knowing I could not fight the racism. That was one evening I didn't eat dinner.

Emerson Gardens

Back in Congressman Van Deerlin's office, I worked hard on helping the Congressman on various legislative issues. I had sent for my son to come to D.C. He was now seven years of age and in elementary school. In 1965, I moved into my own apartment on Emerson Street, N.W. Prior to moving in, I was out walking about six blocks from my residence where I lived with a family. When I saw that two houses had been torn down and an apartment complex was being built, I asked the construction workers if the owner was nearby. He said yes, and pointed him out. Mr. Galvatinas, a Greek man asked me, "And what may I do for you, young lady?" I asked him if I could see the blueprints of the apartment complex he was building. He asked me, "What do you know about blueprints?" I explained to him that I once worked with engineers and architects at General Dynamics and knew that before anything is built, there must be a blue print. He laughed and showed me the blueprints. I told him once the project was completed, I would like an apartment. I pointed out to him the one bedroom/ one den apartment that I wanted. He said, "Get a hundred dollars to me and fill out this application. In September, we will have completed the complex and you may move in." I got the apartment, furnished it, but would not move in until others moved into the apartment building. Also, when someone would move into one of the apartments on my floor.

Shortly after moving into my apartment, I became the Vice President of the Tenants Association at Emerson Gardens, and lived there with my son for over twenty years in peace, until new management took ownership. They realized that I had become a Muslim in the Nation of Islam, with The Honorable Minister Louis Farrakhan. For approximately twelve years or more, I was constantly, in court battles with management, and with each court battle, God allowed me to win. All Praise Is Due To Allah (God).

I dated beautiful, handsome, intelligent men. I always chose men who my son could look up to. I kept the words of Ethel Payne, my Congressman, and Andrew Hatcher, and lived a moral life. My male companions knew they had to respect me and my son. There was no drinking of alcohol or smoking in my home. Wine was allowed every once in a while.

Beauty of the Ghetto

Ernie Barnes, my next door neighbor in San Diego who was instrumental in my becoming a "Chargette" with the San Diego Chargers football team, was a professional artist. He hired me to promote his artwork. He had an exhibit called the "Beauty of the Ghetto." His paintings depicted "Black" folk life. All the drawings were quite unusual, "High Aspirations," "Come Sunday," "Sugar Shack," "The Story Teller," and so many other beautiful works of art. I was then dating Congressman John Conyers, Jr., a young freshman Democratic Congressman from Detroit, Michigan. Congressman Jack Kemp (R-NY), who formerly was a football player with the San Diego Chargers, and a friend of Ernie Barnes agreed, at my asking, to host an art exhibit for Ernie Barnes. Mrs. Ethel Kennedy also became one of the key sponsors. She hosted a luncheon meeting at her home for Ernie and myself. Served at the luncheon meeting was southern fried chicken. I laughed at myself, "White folk will be White folk," Mrs. Kennedy serving fried chicken to her Black guests. Ernie, Ethel Kennedy and I, later sat around her swimming pool to discuss the upcoming art exhibit. Senator Ted Kennedy and several other Congressmen came by and all were quite interested in the P.R. plan I had drafted. The exhibit was scheduled to be held at the Museum of African Art. The Director of the Museum, Warren Robbins, a Jewish man, who had been a curator of African Art Exhibits, responded to my request to have the first "Beauty of the Ghetto" art exhibit at the Museum of African Art. I made him aware that Mrs. Ethel Kennedy, Congressman Jack Kemp, and Congressman John Conyers, Jr. would be the hosts, and that I had written something about Ernie Barnes and his "Beauty of the Ghetto" for Congressman John Conyers, Jr. to submit into the "Extension of Remarks" in the Congressional Record (Wednesday, September 25, 1974). Of course, Warren Robbins saw this as an opportunity for exposure of the Museum of African Art, which was housed in the home of Frederick Douglass on Capitol Hill. The exhibit was a tremendous success, especially with the exposure of such noted personalities, who hosted the exhibit. Warren Robbins asked me to be an advisor to his Board. Later, the Museum of African Art became a part of the Smithsonian Institute, and moved to a larger complex funded by the federal government.

Mrs. Ethel Kennedy also hosted the "Beauty of the Ghetto" in New York at the Bedford-Stuyvesant Cultural Center, where Dr. Franklin Thomas was the director. The exhibit was highly successful. I had worked hard for both exhibits and made acquaintances with so many noted personalities, most of whom praised me for the work I had done and thanked me for getting such noted art as the "Beauty of the Ghetto" recognized. I continued to promote and market Ernie's works of art for several years.

Keep the Faith, Baby

While working with Congressman Van Deerlin, I handled much of the constituent's mail. Quite a bit of mail was coming into the Congressman's office regarding Congressman Adam Clayton Powell, Jr., having his wife on payroll even though she didn't live in his District in New York, nor reside in the District of Columbia. Congressman Powell, in 1944, had become the first Black Congressman from the Eastern Region since Reconstruction. He stood strong for Blacks and the poor, and fought hard against segregation, for Civil Rights and for school integration. Congressman Samuel M. Gibbons, a Democrat from Florida, would come into Congressman Van Deerlin's office many mornings. They would talk with the Congressman's door closed, which was unusual for the Congressman, because he always kept his door open, no matter with whom he was meeting. I, always wanting to be in the know, would keep an ear to what was being discussed between Congressman Van Deerlin and Congressman Gibbons. Both of the Congressmen had thick files on Congressman Powell. Congressman Gibbons and other Congressmen had a dislike for Congressman Adam Clayton Powell. He was the Chairman of the powerful Education and Labor Committee, and was very influential on Capitol Hill. He believed in a good fight, especially against Dixiecrats and lynching.

Congressman Gibbons and others talked Congressman Lionel Van Deerlin into introducing a Resolution into Congress stating that no Congressman could have a clerk hire on their payroll, who didn't either live in their Congressional District or in the District of Columbia.

Congressman Lionel Van Deerlin was a Junior Congressman on the Interstate and Foreign Commerce Committee, Committee on House Administration and Sub-Committee on Communications. He later became Chairman of the Sub-Committee. Shortly after introducing his legislation, it was learned that within the House Rules Committee there was legislation that had been made into law spelling out the same as Congressman Van Deerlin's Resolution. Congressman Adam Clayton Powell was charged with having his wife, who lived in Puerto Rico (not the District of Columbia nor his Congressional District), on his Congressional Payroll. It was said that she was paid a high salary. The media picked it up, and there was a move in Congress to impeach Congressman Powell. His constituents traveled to Washington, D.C. from New York in droves. Many came and would stand outside of Congressman Van Deerlin's office and shout ugly words. Being a Black on his staff, I was called all kinds of names. I received threatening phone calls, and was told that harm's way would befall my son. For a while, I had private police to follow my son to and from school. He was not aware, because I didn't want to frighten him. I was dating Congressman John Conyers, Jr. He and other Black Congressmen told me to quit working for Congressman Van Deerlin. Just walk out of his office and don't return. I told Congressman Conyers and the other Black Congressmen that they had a lot of nerve to express such words to me. I asked Congressman Conyers and the other Congressmen if they had a job for me. I inquired of them, "Who would support me if I quit?" I became very angry and told all of them, including Congressman Conyers, to leave me alone on that subject. I had previously gone to Congressman Powell and told him what Congressman Van Deerlin and others had planned, but he laughed it off and said, "Daughter, they can't touch me." I shared much with his secretary and companion, Corrine Huff, hoping that she could warn Congressman Powell. I went to Congressman Diggs when I first learned of what others were attempting to do against Congressman Powell. He, too, didn't take me seriously.

Congressman Conyers served on the Special Committee of the House Judiciary Committee to unseat Congressman Powell. The Committee he served on recommended to the House, to have Congressman Powell unseated. In 1967, Congress did just that. He was stripped of his seniority and power. Congressman Powell was denied his Congressional seat. As pastor of Harlem's Abyssinian Baptist Church, he had a strong Black Community power base.

"Keep The Faith, Baby!" In 1969, Congressman Powell was re-elected. He regained his Congressional seat, but had no real power on a Committee or Sub-Committee. He left the House of Representatives. The United States Supreme Court had voted to clear Congressman Powell of all charges, based on the fact that racism was the evil force that caused the charge.

Some years later, Congressman Powell became ill and retreated on an island. The relationship with his companion, Corrine Huff, soon dissolved. He later took on another companion, who, after he passed, married Congressman Charles Diggs. Years earlier, he too was unseated by the House of Representatives because he was accused and found guilty on a charge of taking kickbacks from his alleged girlfriend's, who was on his staff, congressional salary.

Friendships In All Walk of Life

Congressman John Conyers, Jr., and Congressman Lionel Van Deerlin became tennis partners and are friends to this day. I continued to date Congressman Conyers, until I realized that the relationship was not going anywhere. The two of us throughout the years, have remained friends. Years later, when I joined the staff of the Honorable Minister Louis Farrakhan, Congressman Conyers could not understand my decision. He questioned me and finally one day, I convinced him to come and listen to Minister Farrakhan. He then began to see what I had been telling him for so many years concerning The Honorable Minister Louis Farrakhan. To date, he is one of Minister Farrakhan's strongest supporters.

Thirty-four years after leaving the Congressman's staff, I was working with Minister Farrakhan who hosted the 2002 "Saviours' Day" in Los Angeles, California. After "Saviours' Day," my sister, Linda Walker and I, drove to San Juan Capistrano, to have lunch with former Congressman Lionel Van Deerlin. The Congressman was quite happy to see us, as we were to see him. When our mother, in 1975, had been brutally murdered (tortured for many hours and body parts chopped off with a hatchet), the Congressman helped me and my son get to California from Washington, D.C., and did all that he could in support of our family. He was a pall-bearer at our mother's funeral. In 1970, when my sister who was eleven months younger than I, was brutally murdered, Congressman Van Deerlin assisted us. He has always been kind to me and my family. I have always felt very much indebted to Congressman Van Deerlin. He has done much for me. Bringing me to Washington, D.C. opened many doors of opportunity in which I have truly benefited.

While at lunch, the Congressman, my sister and I, talked about "old times." One of the things we discussed was the late Congressman Adam Clayton Powell, Jr. Congressman Lionel

Van Deerlin told us that Congressman Powell, in making reference to him in his book, called Van Deerlin "a Republican." Congressman Van Deerlin said that this may have been Congressman
Powell's way of getting back at him. He also told us that an
organization in Los Angeles, California had given a big event in
honor of the late Congressman Adam Clayton Powell, Jr., and
that Congressman Powell's sons (both are named Adam Clayton
Powell), were present. I asked Congressman Van Deerlin how
did the sons treat him. He said both the sons were quite polite
and greeted him warmly. I asked Congressman Van Deerlin if
he knew what had transpired between one of his secretaries and
Congressman Powell. I told the Congressman what the secretary
had told me, and I said to Congressman Van Deerlin, that was the
reason I thought he fought so hard against Congressman Powell.
Congressman Van Deerlin assured me he didn't know of what I
had just told him. He said that he would ask his wife, Mary Jo,
if she had knowledge of what I had shared with him. I believed
Congressman Van Deerlin. Sometimes "secrets" are not sur-
faced, and if they are, it may be years down the road. I said no
more. Congressman Powell is dead, and the secretary, although,
still alive, to our knowledge, had not shared her "secret" with the
Powell family. I said to the Congressman, "Some things are better left alone." He agreed.

New World Orchestra

A t that same 2002 "Saviours' Day," my son and I, along with hundreds of Believers and friends, on my 64th birthday, February 13th, witnessed the Honorable Minister Louis Farrakhan, perform "A Night of Beethoven" with the New World Orchestra . I gave the orchestra it's name at the Minister's first Violin Concert in Chicago, Illinois when he performed the Felix Mendelssohn Violin Concerto conducted by Maestro Michael Morgan. "A Night of Beethoven" was conducted by Maestro David Warble at the Cerritos Center for The Performing Arts. Minister Farrakhan mentioned in his Concert Program Booklet, how I had made contact on his behalf with Mrs. Ayke Agus, author of a book on her teacher, Jascha Heifetz, the famous violinist. Mrs. Agus, after meeting Minister Farrakhan, coached him on six occasions while he was in Phoenix, Arizona, preparing for his Cerritos Concert. She also performed in the New World Orchestra, at Minister Farrakhan's Cerritos Center concert. She was the concertmaster.

The Heavyweight

While in Chicago, on tour with the Ebony Fashion Fair, Mr. John H. Johnson gave a reception at the Palmer House for the Ebony models. I invited my friend, Jerri Spencer. There were so many of "Chicago's Who's Who" present. Mr. Robert (Bob) Johnson, one of the senior executives at Johnson Publications, told me there was someone who wanted to meet me. He brought the gentleman over. It was Muhammad Ali. Herbert Muhammad was with him. Muhammad Ali and I talked. I really didn't know who he was, nor did I know that the father of Herbert Muhammad was The Most Honorable Elijah Muhammad. Muhammad Ali asked me how long I was to be in the city of Chicago. I told him that we had a three day break before continuing on our tour. He asked me if I would have lunch with him. I told him that I was not at the Hotel with some of the other models, but that I was staying at Jerri and Prince Spencer's apartment. Prince Spencer, who was an entertainer was one of "The Step Brothers." He was on the road. I told Muhammad Ali that Jerri and I would accept his invitation. We went to a restaurant. Herbert Muhammad was with us. I ordered a liverwurst sandwich, a salad, and french fries. Muhammad Ali said, "When you are with the champ you order a steak and what you are ordering is pork." I had not thought of what I ordered as pork and felt somewhat embarrassed. I knew nothing about the Muslim religion, their restrictive diet or lifestyle. After lunch, Muhammad Ali invited Jerri Spencer and I to the Roberts Motel where he was staying. He said that he wanted us to hear his song, "The Knockout." Jerri and I went to visit him. Again, Herbert Muhammad was present. We listened to his recording, laughed and talked. Muhammad Ali, as Jerri and I were leaving, stood beside me and said, "You could fit well, I'm looking for a wife, I have to get married." I said to him, "That is not the way you get a wife. There has to be a relationship." They all laughed. In several of the cities on the Ebony Fashion Fair Tour, I would walk out on the ramp, look out into the audience, and there would be Muhammad Ali. Some of the models were quite taken by him. He was always polite and quite mannerable. Herbert Muhammad was always with him.

Once I returned to D.C., I received a phone call at the office from Muhammad Ali. One of the staff persons took the message. When I got to the office, Congressman Van Deerlin called me in his office. He asked me how I was acquainted with Muhammad Ali. I told him we had met during the time I was modeling with Ebony Fashion Fair. We had lunch, were in each other's company; and that, at all times, others were with us. He asked me if I knew anything about the Muslims. He told me there was a lot of controversy regarding Muhammad Ali and his lifestyle. He said that unless I had developed a serious relationship (I had not), he would recommend that I not see him, because to get involved, he didn't think I could handle the situation. I was not romantically involved with Muhammad Ali, so I followed the Congressman's advice and didn't continue to see him.

Safe Keeping

On another occasion, Congressman Van Deerlin became quite protective of me. I had wanted to travel South to a rally where Dr. Martin Luther King, Jr. was speaking. I had met Dr. King's attorney, Henry Arrington from Florida, and one of his young workers, Reverend Walter Fauntroy. I was all ready to head South, and the Congressman told me that I could not take off from work. He told me that he had brought me out of my mother's house to Washington, D.C., and that he was responsible for me. He said, "I know how you are. You get real involved. What if something were to happen to you? That's all I need. The Press, your family and many of my constituents would hold me to blame." I told him, "This is civil rights we are fighting for, and I want to go and hear Dr. King." The Congressman told me that I could fight for civil rights by working hard on Capitol Hill where civil rights laws are passed. Work with him and together we would work to fight for "civil rights". I needed my job. I went and talked with my Priest and told him what the Congressman had said to me. The Priest pointed out to me that the Congressman was right. He did have a responsibility for my safe keeping, and that he, too didn't want to see me travel South to hear Dr. Martin Luther King, Jr. speak. He felt it was taking too much of a risk, especially given all the civil rights disturbances in the South.

Commission on Civil Disorders

A fter the situation with Congressman Adam Clayton Powell, Jr., I looked for a way out of the Congressman's office. God surely hears prayers, for one day, I was reading the <u>Washington Post,</u> and lo and behold, there was a story on President Johnson appointing a Commission on Civil Disorders to study the riots that had been plaguing the country, including the riots in the Nation's Capitol. The President had appointed Governor Otto Kerner of Illinois as the chairman with Mayor John Lindsey of New York as the vice chairman. Some of the commissioners were the president of the N.A.A.C.P., Roy Wilkins, Senator Edward Brooks (R-MA), Mrs. Catherine Peden of Kentucky, the chief of police in Atlanta, Georgia, several congresspersons with whom I was acquainted, and others. I immediately sent a letter to the White House, and through a person on the congressional liaison staff, my letter was gotten to the President. I later received a phone call from Attorney David Ginsburg's office. He had been appointed as the Executive Director of the Commission by President Johnson. I was to come for an interview. As God Wills it, I became the special assistant to the commissioners. The tenure of the commission was for a year. In my departure from Congressman Van Deerlin's office, he thanked me for the years of service. He especially thanked me for my loyalty during the Congressman Adam Clayton Powell, Jr., crisis.

In the Thursday, September 7, 1967, San Diego, California *Independent* newspaper, described as "America's Target Community Newspaper Group", was a front page story:

> *"Local Lady to Aid Group in Riot Study"*—Washington

>> "Claudette M. Johnson, secretary to Rep.
>> Lionel Van Deerlin (D-San Diego), has been named
>> to a key staff post with President Johnson's newly
>> established Commission on Civil Disorders.
>> Miss Johnson took over this week as administra-

tive assistant to David Ginsburg, executive director
of the panel.

The 11-member commission, headed by Governor
Otto Kerner of Illinois, was created by the President on
July 31 to investigate the causes of urban rioting. As a
commission aide, Miss Johnson will take a one-year
leave of absence from her job as a member of Van
Deerlin's Washington staff.

* * *

'I am sorry to lose Miss Johnson, but proud she has
been selected for this important post,' Van Deerlin
said. 'She has been of great assistance to me for the
past five years, and I know she will be just as valuable
an asset to the Commission in the momentous task
it has undertaken.'

* * *

Miss Johnson has been with Van Deerlin since he
first came to Congress in January, 1963. Before joining
the Congressman, she resided for 16 years in San Diego
where she was active in efforts to achieve equal rights.

In 1962, she won a test case against a downtown
San Diego beauty parlor which had refused her service.
Later, she became the first Negro member of the Chargettes,
an all-girl dancing team that performs at home games of the
San Diego Chargers.

A graduate of the John Robert Powers Modeling
School, Miss Johnson also has enjoyed a successful
secondary career as a professional fashion model. In 1963,
she was chosen by *Ebony* magazine as one of 10 young
women to make a national tour with Ebony Fashion Fair."

The work on the Kerner Commission on Civil Disorders was
quite intense. I had previously met Dr. Martin Luther King, Jr.,
and many of the witnesses who testified before the commission.
The majority of the commission staff were White and Jewish,
not many Blacks. The General Counsel was Black. He brought
Nathaniel Jones, his Assistant General Counsel, with him from
Ohio. Nathaniel Jones and I became close friends. I would often
invite him to my apartment for a home-cooked meal. He told
me that I would always be appreciated by him for the kindness I
extended. He later became a Judge for the United States Court

of Appeals for the Sixth Circuit, appointed by President Carter in 1979. Judge Jones retired in 2002.

During one of the luncheon meetings of the Kerner Commission, with the Commissioners, top Commission staff, and some key Government Officials, Mr. Charles (Tex) Thornton, Chairman and C.E.O. of General Dynamics/ Astronautics and one of the Commissioners, made a remark with reference to Blacks. He used the word, "niggras." I sat there and listened as he made his statement, making reference to "niggras" several times. I looked around the room, waiting for one of the other Black commission staff personnel to correct him. No one said a word. Finally, I raised my hand. Mr. David Ginsburg, the executive director of The Commission, seemed reluctant to recognize that I had raised my hand. He finally acknowledged me and looked as if to say, "Don't make waves," as he knew how vocal I was because I had brought to his attention that the Commission was staffed with mostly White and Jewish workers, only a few Blacks. I stood and said to Mr. Thornton, "Sir, I don't mean to be disrespectful, as you have by using the word "niggras" when referencing Negroes..." I told him that he should not ever use that word, but instead use the word Negro or Black, when he is referencing descendants of Africans. Mr. Thornton seemed quite embarrassed. He apologized and said before everyone listening, that in all his years of professional life, no one had ever corrected him and told him that the word, "niggra" was improper to use. He thanked me, and I, listening to his apology, thought, "Yeah right, " He was so use to disrespecting Blacks, he didn't even care how or when he used the word. Mr. Charles (Tex) Thornton, was a Texan and a personal friend to the late President Johnson.

President Johnson, when appointing the Kerner Commission on Civil Disorders, had said to the commissioners, "Let your search be free, as best as you can, find the truth, the whole truth and express it in your report." Those were the words of President Johnson. The commissioners did just as he instructed. However, after reading the Kerner Report, President Johnson sent the report back, and extended the lifespan of the Commission for another six months. He said that the Kerner Report was "too strong", and that "… the American people would be in an uproar. Water the report down." The Kerner Report had stated, "The Nation was moving toward two societies, one Black and one White, separate and unequal." That was in 1968. Has anything really changed for the better? Senator Fred Harris (D-OK), who was a Kerner Commissioner, stated in his and Dr. Lynn A. Curtis' (President of The Milton S. Eisenhower Foundation) 1998 "Millennium Breach" that "People in America need to be aware that things are getting worse, race and poverty are intertwined, and each makes the other worse." Senator Harris was quoted in the <u>Washington Post</u> after the release of the "Millennium Breach," "The Nation's poverty really stopped toward the end of the 1970's, and we began in many ways to go backwards."

Federal City College

After the lifespan of the Kerner Commission, instead of returning on the staff of Congressman Van Deerlin (I had taken a leave of absence), I sought and found a position, Director of Community Outreach, with Federal City College. I was on staff when we first opened our doors in the late 1960's. Federal City College was the first land grant college in an urban city. It was intended to be a model for other urban cities. A land grant college is founded in an agricultural state, not an urban city. My position as Director of Community Outreach, was directly in the vice president's office (Dr. Harland Randolph) with me making a report of our activities to the president (Dr. Frank Farner) once a month.

Monies to operate the college were appropriated by the U.S. Congress (House District Committee) and from private funds. I worked closely with the Representative of the District of Columbia, Congressman Walter Fauntroy, meeting with his staff for support of Federal City College. I developed a Community Outreach Program that was highly successful. Many of my contacts were from the years on Capitol Hill and during the time I had to communicate with witnesses, whom we had to come before the Kerner Commission to testify.

I also set-up programs to help Sam Jones, who came to the college from the Boston Celtics Basketball Team. He had been hired to direct the Athletic Department, and John Thompson, who was the assistant athletic director. John Thompson later became the famous basketball coach of Georgetown University Basketball team in Washington, D.C. I became close friends with Sam and his wife, Gladys. Sam Jones took my son to his basketball camp, where Tony spent an entire summer. Sam didn't charge me one cent. My son learned a lot that summer. I will always be grateful to Sam and his wife, Gladys, for their kindness.

My work was challenging and I learned a lot. In my relationship with Congressman John Conyers, Jr., I convinced him, as one of the leading Members on the Judiciary Committee, to involve Federal City College in holding hearings as it related to the Civil Rights Movement. He did, and the college with our other programs got "on the map" and a lot of attention was brought to the college. One of our community outreach events, jointly with Congressman Conyers, was hosting Sister Fannie Lou Hamer, a dynamic civil rights activist. We hosted a luncheon at Billy Simpson's restaurant. It was a grand affair. In my private talks with Ms. Hamer, she shared with me how she was treated when arrested for being involved in a civil rights demonstration. She said the jailers took cattle prods and put them to her vagina area, which was like an electric shock. She suffered a lot. She was a strong and bold Black sister who was famously quoted as saying, "I'm sick and tired of being sick and tired."

We fought hard and long and eventually, the vice president, Dr. Harland Randolph became president. We began to lobby in Congress for Federal City College to become a University, and praise God it did, becoming the University of the District of Columbia (UDC). Some years later, Dr. Ralph L. Cortada became president. He had been one of the department chairs at Federal City College, and knew of my work. At the encouragement of Congressman Mervyn Dymally (D-CA), Dr. Cortada hired me as a consultant. As a consultant, I functioned in many posts, mainly in student recruitment activities, and acting as liaison between the diplomatic community, U.S. Congress, and the private sector. I also established, at the president's request, policies, procedures and systems to promote a more efficient management, especially between the faculty, board and student body. In the late 1980's, Minister Dr. Abdul Alim Muhammad was the Minister of Mosque #4 in Washington D.C. With his approval, I went to the president of the student body, the chairman of the board and President Cortada to bring the Honorable Minister Louis Farrakhan to the University of the District of Columbia. Of course, there was much controversy, but Allah made us the winner, and Minister Farrakhan spoke at the university, meeting some of the key board members, faculty, staff and student body.

Reverend David Eaton was one of Federal City College's Department Chairs. He took me under his wing. I was like a family member, very close to his family. Years later, I arranged for The Honorable Minister Louis Farrakhan to meet with Reverend David Eaton at his residence in Washington, D.C. He presented the original soundtrack of Minister Farrakhan's musical "The White Man's Heaven Is A Black Man's Hell", which Minister Farrakhan had recorded many years prior, and the original soundtrack had been misplaced. Reverend Eaton has made his transition. He is remembered in our prayers.

Tragedy Strikes

After leaving the University of the District of Columbia, I started my own P.R. Consulting Firm. I experienced some personal tragedies, with my sister, eleven months younger than myself, murdered, and then five years later, my beloved mother brutally murdered.

My sister, Margo, as we called her, was stabbed seven times in the chest area by a deranged former boyfriend. Margo was a registered nurse and an aspiring actress. Her drama teacher was the late Van Whitfield, former husband of the now famous actress Lynn Whitfield, whom he coached and trained to be the actress she is today.

My sister shared with her boyfriend, her time as a nurse, a drama student, single mother, and was so occupied that she didn't want to have a personal relationship. She had moved from her apartment to our aunt's home. It was a Sunday, on Father's Day in Los Angeles, California that my aunt, cousin and other family members went out to dinner. Margo's former boyfriend had been acting "ugly" so my aunt told Margo to lock the doors, and if he came to the house, not to allow him in.

Our young cousin, less than ten years of age was in the house with Margo. A knock on the front door, and there he was, Margo's former boyfriend. He asked her to please let him in so that they could talk. She gave in and opened the door. According to our young cousin, when Margo asked him to leave after they had a heavy debate of her not wanting to go out with him anymore, he said, "If I can't have you, no one will." He began to stab her, and fled from the house. Margo crawled to the telephone and called 911. She was rushed to the hospital, but she passed en route, for the seventh stab pierced one of her heart arteries and she bled to death.

My beloved mother just 55 years of age was extremely loving and kind. She called me in January, 1975. It was late in the evening. I couldn't talk with her, because I had just dreamed the night before of myself in a funeral procession, walking behind a casket. My mother was not beside me in the procession, as she had been at my sister's funeral, just five years prior. The dream frightened me because I realized she was in the casket. In her phone call, she said, "Honey, Kathy's friend is real nice. She brought him to the house over the New Year holiday."

I said in somewhat of an angry voice, "Mother, don't trust any friend of Kathy's. The lifestyle she leads as a substance abuser, no friend of hers will be a friend of yours." I told my mother not to let any friend of Kathy's in her home. My mother then said to me, "Honey, have you dreamed of me in any of your recent dreams?" I got choked up and said, "Mother, I have to go. Goodbye." That was my last conversation with my mother.

The very next evening, I was told that my sister Kathy's friend came to my mother's home. She let him in. He asked for money and when my mother would not give it to him, he forced her to the master bedroom, tortured and abused her, and chopped parts of her body with a hatchet. She didn't make much of a sound, because my young nephew and niece were in the house. When her body was thrown against the bedroom door, my little nephew heard the noise and took himself and his little sister next door, where the neighbor called the police. I later received a phone call to my D.C. residence from my grandmother, who was crying, saying something had happened to her daughter (my mother) and for me to come home. "Oh, please, Claudette, hurry, hurry and come home. The police won't let me in Ernestine's house."

I then remembered my dream. I called my mother's house and asked the policeman if my mother was dead. He would not give me any information. I then called Congressman Van Deerlin and told him my mother was dead, and that he, as a U.S. Congressman, could call my mother's home and get information from the policeman. The Congressman called me back and said, "How did you know that your Mom was dead? The police had not released any information." I told him I just knew and asked if he would arrange for my son and I to fly immediately, first-class to San Diego, California. Congressman Van Deerlin did as I requested. He also came to San Diego and assisted my family. The congressman was a pallbearer at mother's funeral. Even though these were indeed sad times in my life, I kept on keeping on.

Solomon Burke, who not too long ago, was inducted into the Music Hall of Fame, was a dear friend to me and my sister, Patricia Edwards. He came to San Diego to be with our family and attended our mother's funeral. He was one of the pallbearers. Our family will always be indebted to him for his kindness and support.

We Meet Again

Throughout the years, Congressman Conyers and I have remained friends. He would call and invite me to various social events. One such event was a reception for Don King, the boxing promoter, held at the home of the Senegalese Ambassador. At the reception, I saw a woman I had befriended when we both were involved in IRMA (International Retail Marketing Association). The woman was an American Indian, by the name of Wauneta Lonewolf. Upon meeting her, I thought she was Black, until one day she explained her heritage. We both had something in common, because of my American Indian heritage. Wauneta told me of the work she was doing with Muhammad Ali and Don King. Don King and I met at the reception. I told him I knew Wauneta from years ago. He asked me to come out to Maryland, because he wanted to hire me to assist him. We did meet, and Don King told me what he wanted me to do: Find a motel for Muhammad Ali's sparring partners who helped him to train; find a good photographer; set-up a meeting for him with the Congressional Black Caucus; arrange a meeting for him to meet the Governor of Maryland; coordinate a reception he wanted to host for Muhammad Ali; and arrange for interviews. Don King told me of the past criminal charges against him, and that the court could not accept his wife's testimony (a wife cannot testify against her husband). He knew of my connections on Capitol Hill. I told him that a meeting could be arranged for him and the Speaker of the House, Tip O'Neal. Perhaps through the Speaker of the House, he could get a Presidential Pardon. Don King met with the Congressional Black Caucus (C.B.C.). I arranged the meeting with its chairman, Congressman Andrew Young (D-GA). At the meeting, Don King invited the C.B.C. to come and meet Muhammad Ali. The only one who came was Congresswoman Yvonne Braithwaite (D-CA), of Los Angeles, California. None of the other Black Caucus Members would come close to Muhammad Ali. I coordinated a beautiful reception for Muhammad Ali, hosted by Don King at the Embassy Row Hotel in Washington, D.C. The Speaker of the House did attend. Later, I arranged for Don King to meet the Speaker. He had agreed to help Don King in terms of getting a Presidential Pardon, although I learned from Don King years later that the pardon was never granted. At one of the sparring matches, Muhammad Ali asked me, "Where are you from, don't I know you?" He had forgotten meeting me some ten to eleven years earlier. Muhammad Ali went on to win the Ali/Young fight in Landover, Maryland.

Family

Acreage Home Community
The Happy Young Years of me and my siblings.

2124 Paul Quinn
The home of my uncle and aunt, Richard and Bell
Cebrun "The Happy Years"

Me and my sister, Margurite Ann. She was 11 months
younger than I. Her birth anniversary was February 1st,
mine February 13th. Margurite was brutally murdered
in 1970.

My son, Anthony LaMare as an infant; my mother,
Ernestine Edith; my grandmother, Margurite; and
myself

My son, Anthony LaMare at 6 months of age

Anthony LaMare – 'My Blessing'

FAMILY

Me and my beloved son Anthony LaMare

My granddaughter, Tiffany Mayo; my son, Anthony; and me.

My sisters Patricia Bell, Linda Joyce, and me

The Johnson siblings
Seven of my Brothers and Sisters are not on the photo

My Spiritual Daughter Rahtsiyah Baht Ammi and me

My Spiritual Daughter Hoshannah Baht Israel and me

FAMILY

My Spiritual Son and Daughter Immanuel and Elianah Ivrahim

My God Son Karenda Scott Bryant

My spiritual son and daughter, Thomas and Sharon Muhammad

My God Son, Travis Alexander Bryant

COMING OUT

1956 'Presented to Society' – Debutante Ball

1962 San Diego Chargettes

EBONY FASHION FAIR

Jet magazine cover, "Congressional Secretary is Fashion Fair Model' (October 3, 1963)

Miss Alaga U.S.A. says:

"I'm sure Alaga is your favorite syrup, too."

Lovely Claudette Johnson, dressed in her striking Alaga Syrup Hostess Gown, is the picture of elegance. A fashion model and secretary to a member of Congress, Miss Johnson has always loved the rich, field-fresh flavor of Alaga real Ribbon Cane Syrup.

MAPLE FLAVORED— RIBBON CANE FLAVORED

Commercial Model –"Alaga Syrup" - 1963

Ebony Fashion Fair – 1963

Congressman Lionel Van Deerlin (D-37ᵗʰ District now Retired) and me

Congressman John Conyers, Jr. (D-MI) and me at the 2ⁿᵈ Congressional Black Caucus Dinner

Congressman Paul Findley (D-IL) 1964

Women on Capitol Hill: Former Congresswoman Carrie Meeks (D-FL), Former Congresswoman Eva Clayton (D-NC), Congresswoman Carolyn Cheeks Kilpatrick (D-MI)

BEAUTY OF THE GHETTO

Me, The Artist Ernie Barnes and Mrs. Ethel Kennedy, "The Beauty of the Ghetto" Art Exhibit at the Frederick Douglass Museum, Washington, DC

The late Wauneta Lonewolf, Muhammad Ali and me presenting "The Beauty of the Ghetto" portfolio

Mrs. Ethel Kennedy and me at "Beauty of the Ghetto"

THE PRESIDENT'S COMMISSION ON CIVIL DISORDERS

The Kerner Commission
President Lyndon B. Johnson, signing the President's Commission on Civil Disorders Report

CHINA

Women's World Conference – Beijing, China

The Great Wall of China

1st Lady of the Nation of Islam, Mrs. Khadijah Farrakhan;
Mother Tynnetta Muhammad; Captain Karriemah
Muhammad; and me

The Holy Land - Israel

New World Passover - Dimona, Israel with the Hebrew Israelites

The Honorable Ben Ammi Ben Israel, the Spiritual Leader of the Hebrew Israelites

Ambassador Asiel Ben Israel-Members of his family and me

Hebrew Israelites Sister and Brothers, and me in Tiberias

Hebrew Israelites and Delegation from Asia in Jerusalem

Hebrew Israelite Sisters and me in Dimona, Israel

THE HOLY LAND - ISRAEL

Me on a cruise – The Jordan River

Me in Capernaum

A Bedouin Family – The City of Rahat Black Arab Moslems

The Imam and Deputy Mayor of the Bedouin Ishmaelites and me

Bedouin Ishmaelite children

Me presenting the Bedouin Ishmaelites a video of the Honorable Minister Louis Farrakhan and a *Final Call* newspaper. Our Hebrew Brother was my guide.

The Holy Land - Israel

Bedouin Ishmaelite Family – city of Rahat

Sultan Abu Emammar, The Principal, his two assistants, Ark Urie Ben Nasik Rahm, my Hebrew Guide who is a Professor of English, Arab, Hebrew and History.

Me with the children in the Bedouin School

AFRICA

Nation of Islam International Convention – 1994 Ghana, West Africa

President Jerry John Rawlings and the Honorable Minister Louis Farrakhan

President Jerry John Rawlings; His Protocol Director, Mr. Harry Blavo; and me

King Osabarima Mbra of Oguaa. The oldest reigning King of the Western Region of Ghana

Mother Tynnetta Muhammad and me at the Slave Dungeon in Elmina, Ghana

AFRICA

Visiting a village in Dimbroukro Ivory Coast, West Africa

Nana Bangin and his Family who are descendants of the Herbert Kewku family of Cape Coast, Ghana from 1471.

The Ashanti King, His Majesty Otumfuo Osei Tutu II at the Atlanta, Georgia-Ghana Expo, and Dr. Erieka Bennett of Ghana.

Colonel Muammar Qaddafi - Libya, North Africa

NATIONAL COUNCIL OF NEGRO WOMEN

Supreme Captain, Mustapha Farrakhan; 1st Lady of the Nation of Islam, Mrs. Khadijah Farrakhan; The Honorable Minister Louis Farrakhan; Dr. Dorothy Height; Former V.P. of NCNW, Dr. Jane Smith; me; and Minister Abdul Khadir Muhammad

Dr. Dorothy Height, NCNW Chair Emeritus and me

Honorable Minister Louis Farrakhan; Dr. Dorothy Height; Mrs. Khadijah Farrakhan; and me

ISLAM

Al Asqua Mosque "Dome of the Rock" Jerusalem, Israel

Islamic Flag in background as I sit in posture of contemplation in foreground

El-Bahri Mosque in Tiberias

Me at Mosque Maryam National Headquarters of the Nation of Islam Chicago, Illinois

Mosque of Paris, France

Muhammad Ali and me at Mosque Maryam

GOVERNOR'S COMMISSION ON DISCRIMINATION AND HATE CRIMES

Govenor Rod Blagojevich and me

Farrakhan aide: Panel fallout 'ridiculous'

—BRIAN JACKSON/SUN-TIMES

Claudette Muhammad said Tuesday on WVON-AM radio that she shouldn't be condemned for Farrakhan's remarks. Meanwhile, a fifth member of the governor's anti-discrimination commission said he will resign. STORY BY DAVE MCKINNEY, DAVE NEWBART AND MONIFA THOMAS, PAGE 3

The Missing Link

During a visit to New York, with a friend, I was shopping in Saks Fifth Avenue. I noticed a White man looking at me. He and his wife were together. He came over, introduced himself, and said that he and his wife were close friends and business associates of Senator A. B. Tolbert, a son of President Tolbert of Liberia. He asked me my name and gave me his business card. He told me that A. B. Tolbert was staying at the Ritz Hotel and would I mind if he would tell A. B. Tolbert how to reach me. I thought they were telling the truth. I told my friend who was accompanying me, that the couple seemed honest. My friend didn't like the idea of me telling the gentleman how A. B. Tolbert could reach me. A. B. Tolbert and I did meet. My friend and I had lunch with him. He shared with me the names of his brothers and sisters and told me that I reminded him of his sisters. He then told me who the man was whom I had met at Saks Fifth Avenue. He was a wealthy businessman from South Africa, who had been doing business with the Liberian Government for years. He called A. B. Tolbert and told him that he had met a beautiful Black American woman. He wanted A. B. Tolbert to meet me, because he was helping the President in finding a wife for A. B. My friend and I laughed as A. B. told us the story. After returning to D.C., I was contacted by the Ambassador of Liberia. A. B. had called and told him about me. The Liberian Ambassador was Dean of the Washington, D.C. Diplomatic Corp. He hired me to assist him with President Ford's invitation to the President of Liberia for a State visit to the U. S. This opened up a whole new world of opportunity for me.

My soul is linked to Africa. Although my family tree has been traced to the Portuguese, the Spanish, the French, the Irish and to the American Indian, the predominant ancestral heritage is from "Mother Africa". I am an African born in America, of course not by choice, but by design. The architectural blueprint for this design was purposely made, affording me the occurrence to share the life of my brothers and sisters on both sides of the globe.

The opportunity for me to visit my ancestral homeland came at a time when I was fully prepared. My son was off to college and the responsibility of parenthood had somewhat lifted. An invitation had arrived several months prior to his graduation for me to come to Monrovia, Liberia to be in the wedding of Cietta Tolbert, niece of the late President William Tolbert of Liberia. Her father, Steve Tolbert, the Foreign Minister, was the brother to President Tolbert. Most of my dreams concerning "Mother Africa" would soon materialize. The day of June 17, 1977, I was one of the happiest women on planet earth. My Pan-Am flight from New York was landing at Robert's Field and I was about to embark on a new chapter in my life. As I stepped off the plane, I could feel the rushing heat of the day. The sun was blazing hot, and the weather humid, but neither the heat nor the humidity could dampen my spirit. I was in the fair and majestic land of my dreams.

With my first step on African soil, a feeling of completeness overcame me. It was a sensation I had never before experienced. The missing link for the chain of my nice life was finally put into place. I was whole for the first time in my life. My heart was bursting with joy as I looked into the heavens, singing praise to the Creator for bringing me home.

After greetings of welcome, embracing old friends whom I had last seen in America, and meeting my host's family, we collected my luggage and left from the airport. The drive to the city took well over two hours. The countryside was like a landscape from a painting. The rubber trees, as far as my eyes could see, were standing tall, and the plants and foliage were all shapes, sizes and colors. The beautiful hues of green blended with lovely shades of blue as the greenery danced along the skyline. The air was fresh and clean and smelled sweet. Watching the people as we drove along the roadside, I saw an infinite variety of rich skintones- brown with strokes of violet, pink, red and yellow, mixed in their skin color. The women wore the traditional dress, wrapped in the fashion of their tribe. The fabrics, of different designs and color mixtures, were brilliant and striking.

The infants were carried on the backs of their mothers, who, at the same time, walked with heavy firewood for the day perched atop their heads. In all the countries I visited in West Africa, the women carried a heavy load of either food, firewood, children or materials. The men rejected anything considered "women's work". They even refused to go to the market.

After ten days, I left Liberia for Ghana. The day prior to my departure, I spent many long hours at the Executive Mansion visiting with the late President Tolbert. As I previously mentioned, I first met President Tolbert in June of 1976, in the U.S. during the year of our bicentennial. He was on a state visit at the invitation of former President Ford (Liberia is considered a sister state to America). Those hours spent at the Executive Mansion with the late President helped me to gain a better understanding of the peoples of Africa. He discussed with me, not only the history of his country, but also of the many other countries as well and the complex problems which have sprung from the problems of development towards modernization. He helped me understand the problems of Africa and the problems he was facing as ruler of his own country, that was founded by freed slaves from America. He presented me with a gift of a two volume set of his *Presidential Papers*, which I shall hold very dear because he was assassinated, and I have something concrete other than abstract memories to remember him. I became very close to the Tolbert family. President Tolbert arranged for me to be received by his Ambassadors of each African country I visited, all of whom treated me with extreme kindness.

Ghana is called the "Gold Coast" of West Africa. There was so much to see and I had to see it all in eight days. Everyday was a class in history as I toured the country, going to places I had read about when reading the history of this once very powerful country. A country which was considered the most powerful empire of all West Africa because of its immense wealth and strength of its army. The great late President of Ghana, Kwame Nkrumah, who organized his countrymen toward nationalism, led Ghana to freedom from under British rule, and is recorded in history as one of the most unique persons of all time. He led his country in the fight against poverty, illiteracy and disease and on July 1, 1960, the world watched as he was sworn in as the President of a first sovereign and unitary republic in Africa.

In Accra, Ghana, West Africa, I stayed with Bishop Herbert Kraku and his family. He was the Bishop in the Church Universal and Triumphant of the Ascended Masters' Teachings. I had met Bishop Kraku, his wife and another Ghanaian woman while I was in California attending the University of the Church Universal and Triumphant, chaired by Elizabeth Clare Prophet, who was the head of the church in which Bishop Kraku belonged.

I traveled with Bishop Kraku and his wife, JoAnnah, visiting his wife's village which was nearby Elmina. One chief gave me a pouch with gold nuggets. I was presented with gifts practically everywhere I went.

Elmina, Ghana is a quiet little seashore town I found to be quite historical. Christoforo Colombo (birth given name of Christopher Columbus) stopped there in 1492 (long before the slave trade), on his voyage prior to discovering the New World. While there, he stayed at the Elmina Castle, which had been built in 1482, as a permanent trading post by Portuguese navigators (who came to Ghana seeking gold, ivory and spices). The history books recorded that Blacks came to this country only as slaves. However, when Christopher Columbus departed from Elmina, Ghana, he took with him many Ghanaians—most of whom were learned men with many talents. They were mathematicians, navigators, craftsmen, carpenters, and seamen. Many of the women who accompanied the crew were talented in crafts, pottery design, sewing and weaving and designing fabrics. Visiting the castle, I could feel the vibrations of history. Walking through the castle (now a museum), I observed the restored articles from Christopher Columbus' personal belongings. A ship's log with dates, and an agreement between Columbus and the head of state that the citizens of Elmina could leave with his fleet of vessels, was signed by both parties. Seeing documented evidence of those past historical events caused me to think that perhaps some of the Africans leaving for the New World had not been subjected to the brutality that existed later during the slave trade.

Seventeen years later, after my first visit to Africa, on a trip to Ghana "Saviours' Day" in October 1994, Minister Farrakhan took over 1000 Believers to Accra, Ghana, where "Saviours' Day" was hosted by President Jerry John Rawlings. The Honorable Ben Ammi Ben Israel of The Hebrew Israelites was among The Honorable Minister Louis Farrakhan's many invited guests. It was quite a historical site to witness Ben Ammi, the Hebrews and Muslims walking out from the Chamber of "No Return" in Elmina Castle. It was a sight to see all the many Blacks from various parts of the world, joining Minister Farrakhan in Africa.

I visited the residence of the Head of State, General Acheampong and his wife. We had dinner and discussed the affairs of Ghana. The General and his wife were very pleasant, but I somewhat felt a sense of sadness. The country was under military rule and many Ghanaians were unhappy with the present conditions. Within a year after my visit, General Acheampong was overthrown by a military uprising, thrown into prison and later shot to death.

I traveled to Kumasi, Ghana, the capital city of the Asante Kingdom, where I was blessed to meet the Ashanti King, who was the 15th in a royal line of Asantehenes, which began with His Majesty Nana Osei Tutu I, in 1680. I went to the King's Manhya Palace, stood at the gate and told his security to please take a message to the Ashanti King to let him know that an American woman had traveled to Ghana at her own expense, and that she had rode by public bus from Accra to Kumasi to meet him. I gave the security personnel my name and passport number. After about an hour, one of the King's officials came out to greet me. He told me that I was cleared. After learning of how I traveled to Kumasi, His Majesty the Ashanti King Na'Na received me. I was led into a spacious room, and stood about ten minutes and finally the Ashanti King came out to meet me. He was a pleasant man who greeted me warmly. We talked for about thirty minutes. He took me in a smaller room and showed me the "Golden Stool of the Ashanti Kings", where Ashanti Kings had sat one after another for centuries. He told me that their tradition would be broken by his allowing me to sit on the "stool." He then presented me with Kente cloth which he had recently approved for distribution. He told me that because I had a love for the people of Africa, and had taken time on my own to come to Kumasi, I would be blessed for the rest of my days. He blessed me and told me never to forget Africa. Twenty-seven years later, I met his nephew, His Majesty, Otumfuo Osei Tutu II, who had become the 16th King of the Ashanti in 1999. The meeting took place in Atlanta, Georgia, in September of 2004 at the Ghana Expo, where myself and Minister Abdul Akbar Muhammad represented the Honorable Minister Louis Farrakhan.

I stayed in Kumasi for several days. I went to villages and visited the people. I walked, took the bus and sometimes a cab to get around the city and small villages. Back in Accra, I shared with Bishop Kraku and his family all that I had experienced with the Asantehene. They were amazed because they said no one just came to the King's Palace and gets admitted without an approved appointment. They were so happy for me and told me as the Asantehene had said, I would be blessed for the rest of my days.

Leaving Ghana with my heart filled with treasures that will remain for an eternity, I traveled by car heading for Nigeria, with Bishop Kraku and his wife. We drove along the coast, passing through Togo and Benin, we stopped at villages in each country, drinking palm juice, freshly drained from the palm trees, which made me sleepy. We would pull to the side of the road and get a few hours sleep, always awakening to the sound of children's laughter. They would come and surround the car waiting for us to wake up, only to begin a form of dialogue that was much to their amusement. Stumbling through my words of broken French, I would earnestly try to speak to them. All of whom, as I realized spoke their own tribal dialect. Although, the children nor I could speak the other's language, we did have a form of communication because we were "in tune" with one another. Bishop Kraku and his wife found joy in watching me doing my best to communicate with those we met. We continued our drive to Nigeria, taking in the sights which are still photographed in my mind.

Nigeria is one of the wealthiest countries in West Africa. Lagos, the capital, overflows with people who seem to take very little observation of one another. Most of my time was spent in Elkeja, a small suburb near the airport. My hosts were Captain Thahil and his lovely wife, Esther, who were close friends of Bishop Kraku and his wife. The captain was director of Nigerian Airways. They spent a considerable amount of time in terms of assisting me with the history of Nigeria, of which the majority of human behavior attitudes in Nigeria is based. Much of my time was spent in the homes of friends, who gave dinner parties in my honor. My stay in Nigeria was much in contrast to the other countries I visited.

After leaving Nigeria, I flew to Cote d'Ivore (the Ivory Coast), formerly named the Coast of The King People, a brotherly country, peaceful and wise. It has adjusted to the audacious modernism and the secular traditions in a well-balanced expansion. Abidjan, the capital, is pure utopia. In fact, very few towns in all of West Africa, offer so much diversity. It's a town and a world: from Cocody to Treichville, from Marcory to the Plateau, from Adjame to Vridi. There are streets on the Plateau, the city's business centre that have a daring, aggressive beauty. Treichville, Africa as it was yesterday; Cocody, the residential quarters, dream-like villas nestle in the Hotel Ivoire, with its miniature lake, swimming pool and bar, shops and movie houses, casino, ice-skating rink, tennis courts, golf course; and Toit d'Abidjan, an exclusive restaurant on the 24th floor overlooking the city. Abidjan reminds me, all at once, of Manhattan and its skyscrapers, Paris and its sidewalk cafés, Miami and its water skiing and sailing clubs, and St. Croix and its big game fishing. In the center of this modern, bustling city, one suddenly comes upon the extraordinary, noisy and colorful market, where the goods count for less than the way they are sold.

In the heart of Black Africa, Abidjan offers all the modern entertainments. In the night clubs African rhythms boom outside by side with the best of Western jazz. In addition to restaurants specializing in local fare—sauce Claire, sauce grain, adjaka, plantain, peanut sauce over fish or meat dishes, foo-foo (made from plantain and cassava), and potato-greens over rice—there are restaurants that offer cooking from all over the world. My host wanted to entertain me in the fashion of the city. Myriad lights glittered from the many night clubs, tempting me to agree. I chose, rather, to spend much of my time up-country.

Riding High

M y host introduced me to a very kind and sensitive man, Dr. Kouma Kanga, who is one of the few neurosurgeons in West Africa. I was quite fond of him. Although Dr. Kanga is an urban, westernized African, he proudly told me that he comes out of a traditional background and can trace his roots back to his ancestral village. I told him that one of my reasons for coming to Africa was to learn about the people of my ancestral homeland. To understand Africa, he told me that I must first understand traditional life; it is the source, and the preserver of African culture. With the understanding of African traditional life, I would also discover more about myself. He explained that each culture has its own values, and it should be judged, if at all, by how well it lives up to them.

Several days later, Dr. Kanga drove me to his village, which is about a four-hour drive from Abidjan, located in the central part of the country. The drive afforded me the opportunity to see much of the countryside. Magical, confusing, mysterious and beautiful, vast Greenland stretched as far as the eye could see. The sun setting behind the hills as evening approached, Gauguin could not have painted a more artistic masterpiece, throwing out sun rays that reflected hues of orange, rust, yellow, purple and deep violet. A land of legends and traditions, holding an exceptional cultural heritage.

Feeling the cool breeze rushing against my face and listening to Dr. Kanga, telling the story on the history of his people, as we continued our drive, was a monumental experience for me. The emotions I felt were beyond what I can put into words. The echoes from the past of hundreds and hundreds of years ago, lifted me far above the height of Mount Everest.

He told me that his people are called Aboule and are members of the Akan Clan. Of course his story cannot be documented by written material. Like most African history, the story was to pass, orally and aurally, from one generation to the other, from father to son, through the ages. Naturally, with the years going by and each older person telling a younger person what he remembers being told, stories can get a little mixed up and changed. However, what Dr. Kanga knew is still a good clue to the truth of how his people came to be.

The Akan begins around the fifth century A.D. (five hundred years after the birth of Christ) during the time of the South West Sudan Empire. Within this empire were many sub-regions, Ghana, Mali and Songhai. Several hundred years later, the Moslem religion began to spread from Mecca, one of the capitals of Saudi Arabia, throughout the Arab world. The religion spread across North Africa to the shores of the Atlantic Ocean and became an important and powerful influence in North Africa. The Moslem religion soon crossed the Sahara Desert of West Africa. The men who brought the religion to West Africa were often traders. They came to a number of strong states and empires. Of these strong states, the most important was Ghana, whose capital city at this time was Koumbi, a big city of many thousands of people. The most powerful people in the Ghana region were the Ashanti. The king was known as the ghana or ruler.

This nation was a great trader in gold and quite powerful. The Ashanti had swords and lances made of iron which helped to win wars against neighbors who did not know the use of iron, and who fought with bars of ebony. They learned to make iron tools and how to use such tools to produce more food, another way in which they became stronger than their neighbors. Gradually, the wars became religious ones. The Ashanti fought against the Moslems, who grew in number as a result of the booming trade for salt and other foreign goods. Several chiefs within the Ashanti Kingdom also began to dispute and there was much rivalry between them. There were many setbacks and disasters with so much business dealings, and at the same time, trying to bring about a system of law and order to this land. These chiefs moved to other areas within the Ghana Empire, while others broke away completely, traveling toward the Camoé River to a new land. Those that separated from the Ashanti Kingdom were also a section of the Akan. They had various ethnic backgrounds, all formerly speaking the common Ashanti language.

Many of the tribes within the Akan clan spoke the same dialect called "Tawue".

The Camoé River is the first large river separating Ghana from the new land. When the tribes came to the river, the Priest-King (the religious leader) told the people what had been revealed to him in a dream. He announced that the river needed an infant child, and for the people to cross over safely, they would have to sacrifice a baby. Rivers were worshipped at that time and even today about forty percent of Ivorians are Animist (worshipers of trees, rivers, and various forms of nature). The baby that the river needed was the Queen's only child. She had to make the sacrifice of her beloved son, so that thousands of people could cross the river safely. Throwing her baby in the river, she cried, "bau-oula", meaning "my child is dead". (Bau-child and oula-dead) To this day, that tribe is called the Baoule. Safely crossing the river, the Baoule, the Agni, and several other tribes traveled to the new land—"The Land of Kind People".

Many tribes were already in this "Land of Kind People". They had come from the Mali Empire, North Songhay and from as far off as Tekhur (now Guinea). The Agni stayed near the river, expanding in size along the coast, establishing cities which grew and prospered. The Baoule moved on and settled in the central part of the country. They established Bouaké, Dimbroukro (Dr. Kanga's home), Bouaflé, Katiola, Toumodi and Yamoussoukro (home of President Houphouet-Boigny). The Baoule and the Agri were the largest and most powerful tribes in the "Land of The Kind People". Throughout the years they maintained their power because they respected the system of hierarchy and fol-lowed the rules of their leaders. For a long time these two tribes were the economic lung of the "Land of Kind People".

Prior to colonization by the French in 1893, the "Land of Kind People" had many kingdoms, Baoule, Agni, Senoufo, Ma-linke, and many others. After the country was colonized, it was united and renamed Cote' d'Ivore (the Ivory Coast). This name came from the French because of the large number of elephant herds, which supplied an enormous almost inexhaustible amount of ivory. The capital was Grand-Bassam, located at the mouth

of the Camoé River. It remained the capital until 1899. Binger-
ville, only a couple hundred miles away, was chosen as the capital from 1900 to 1934. Until independence in 1960, the country
was part of a confederation, with eight other countries, Senegal,
Mali, Niger, Dahomey, Guinea, Upper Volta, Mauritania and
Sunda Francias, all belonging to France.

Given its independence by President De Gaulle of France,
the Ivorian government broke away from the confederation,
held elections and voted for a new government, one that gave
the country a new head of state. The Bauole demonstrated their
power—coming together with members of the Akan clan and
many other ethnic groups, they elected Felix Houphouet-Boigny,
President. He held that office since November 27, 1960, being
re-elected by the people in 1965, 1970, 1975, and 1980, and remained President until his death. A man of great political wisdom, a Baoule.

We were approaching Dr. Kanga's village just as he was
finishing his story, and I was still high above Mount Everest.
Taking in such richness of one's culture was an amazing experience. We were met by the village children, who all expressed
their welcome. Children of all ages. Some with swollen stom-
achs, some showing signs of sickness, some with smiles that
melted your heart and some who came to touch me or to hold
my hand giving me a gesture of love. As we toured the village
watching the people and seeing how their lives were structured I
was pleased to see the unity, the extended family of uncles, aunts,
cousins, and grandparents, all sharing in the responsibility of the
children with almost as much authority over the children as the
"real" parents. The older people are the most valued because of
the wisdom they have accumulated in their long lives. There are
no "old folks' homes", and no one tries to get older people "out
of the way". The children have a sense of direction from a very
early age. They are taught, almost from birth, the rules of their
culture, and inherit a lifetime membership in a very large family
that has all the companionship that a family can bring. Loneliness which leads to so many social ills in the Western World is
not a problem in Africa. I questioned why the Western World

often thinks of these people as savages and themselves as civilized. Toward the end of the day, I was taken to the home of the chief. He was an old man, half-blind, but with a very keen sense of awareness. We talked, with Dr. Kanga acting as an interpreter. Although French is the official language of the Ivory Coast, the chief spoke in his tribal language, Baoule. I felt a sense of close kinship to these particular people. They were so humble, living with little of life's necessities. I imagined what it felt like those hundreds of years ago, when their forefathers, who could well have been sisters and brothers of my forefathers, were taken by force, separated and taken to a foreign land. The pain and loneliness of being uprooted from their homes, their children and loved ones taken away, never to see them again, having to submit to a culture, which I am sure seemed barbaric to them. I cried as I stood there among those people; for the many souls that were taken by force to a foreign land, for those who had been left behind, and for the offspring of generations who, like myself, are in America and even others who are scattered around the globe, and know so little about one another. Dr. Kanga dried my tears and told me not to cry. He told me what I had seen was nothing to cry about and that in Africa, people were strong; tears could not undo all the damage done to both his people and mine; I should take what knowledge I had gained from my travels in Africa and utilize it. I should work to create a better understanding among those people who wanted to reach out and help underdeveloped countries. I looked at this man and thought, "Look what he has come from and what he has become, a village boy, who walked miles and miles every day to get his education, and now one of the top neurosurgeons of West Africa." My heart went out to him.

Dr. Kanga asked me to consider being his wife. He told me that he had been married twice before, once in his early age to a woman from his village. The second marriage was to one of the Ivory Coast President's goddaughters. I said that I would think about his proposal because I had a deep feeling for him, and that I would soon return. A year later, I returned.

After leaving the Ivory Coast, I flew to Sierra Leone, staying for a brief visit, and then on to the Gambia. Immediately upon arriving in Banjul, I went to Juffere, the home of Alex Haley's ancestors, presenting gifts to the Chief from the Haley family, George and Doris Haley. George, some years later, became the U.S. Ambassador to the Gambia. There was a ceremony with all the people of the village attending. I was shown many of the places mentioned in Mr. Haley's book, meeting some of the people with whom he had spoken while doing the research for *Roots*. I was taken to the mosque in the center of the village and we all communed in prayer, indeed an inspirational experience, for I thoroughly enjoy learning of all forms of religion. My stay in the Gambia was quite rewarding.

Dakar, Senegal. The Kamara's were perfect hosts. Although they didn't speak English and I spoke very little French, we communicated very well, especially when their sister Ami came to visit. She spoke English fluently. On my second day in Senegal, I was taken by boat to Goree Island. The boat ride was about an hour long. My friends and I took pictures, and they explained the story of the Island to me. Approaching the Island, I could feel vibrations of hostility, poured over from hundred of years ago by the natives who had been held captive there. These natives were brought in bondage to the island from all parts of Central and West African countries and held there until ships from England, France, America, Portugal, Spain and Holland came to take them away to the various parts of the world and sold as slaves. Landing on the island, I was taken to the home of a French lady who was the artist-in-residence (as she was called), and shown many historical papers and pictures which she had collected over the years on the slave trade. She was a close friend to my host. The island has an attractive hotel near the beach where many foreigners come for vacation with small restaurants and boutiques of interest. The people on the island, whose families have lived there for generations, are beautiful. They are a mixture of the African and Europeans who came many centuries ago during the slave trade. Going deeper into the Island, seeing the old ruins, actually going to the caves (slave holds), where the natives were held in bondage, and seeing the shackles and chains and carvings on the walls by the men who had been held in misery, caused me to become violently ill (being extremely sensitive, I can pick up on the slightest vibration). I departed the island with a heavy heart.

I visited Rufeskee, the city where my friend, the late Marvin Gaye, had asked me to locate his family. He told me that one of his fans had traced his family tree to this seaport town. After four hours of going to various families telling them of my search, we finally located the Gaye family that was kin to Marvin Gaye. Hanging on the wall of that Gaye family home was a huge picture of an old woman who looked like the twin of Marvin's father. After taking pictures of the photo and of the family and giving them albums by Marvin, I headed back to Dakar. After returning to the States, I called Marvin, to tell him the good fortune of locating his family and that I had pictures for his scrapbook. He was jubilant.

I took a picture of the photo, had it blown up, and mailed it to Marvin Gaye. He thanked me. Marvin was a gifted and special person. May Allah (God) always Be Pleased with him. I loved my brother Marvin Gaye. When he visited me in D.C., the whole neighborhood came to my apartment complex. Marvin Gaye is here! He would smile and wave at the people. People in D.C. loved him.

Bidding farewell to my host and the many who came to the airport to see me off, and thanking everyone for their kindness, I boarded the plane, took my last look at their smiling faces, and vowed to myself, "Mother Africa, your daughter will return." The plane took off heading for the States via Paris. I reclined my seat, reared back and shut my eyes and thought, what an experience these two months have been, sharing new discoveries of certain parts of West Africa, its people, and at the same time, discovering a lot about myself. These discoveries are not gained from reading history books or from the media, but from real life experiences—experiences that will be with me for an eternity. All of which were good, given to me by God, who is always on time. I was thankful to "Mother Africa".

Presidential Election

The Presidential election had put President-Elect Carter as the new President of the United States. Chester Carter, an acquaintance, was the Deputy Chief of Protocol under Ambassador Shirley Temple-Black. She was the Chief of Protocol of the U.S., and former American Ambassador to Ghana. Chester Carter took leave of his post as The Deputy Chief of Protocol, to become the Director of Protocol for the President-Elect Carter's inauguration. He asked me to come on-board as a volunteer. After many weeks of volunteering, I was hired as an Assistant Deputy to the Director of Protocol. I worked with members of the Diplomatic Corps, and was in charge during the inauguration activities of the Blair House that accommodated members of the Diplomatic Corps and Foreign Representatives of State, who came to the U.S. for President-Elect Carter's inauguration. These visitors all represented their government. It was a great challenge for me. I met a lot of people from various countries, learning the cultural climate of the many countries. The inaugural activities were well attended. After his inauguration, President Carter wrote a personal letter to me and sent me an autographed photo of himself, thanking me for the hard work, and over 100 hours of volunteer service, before I was given a salaried position.

Return on a Promise

I sent my son, after his high school graduation, off to Morehouse College, arranged for a friend to stay in my apartment, packed up, keeping my promise to Dr. Kanga, and went back to the Ivory Coast, West Africa. I loved it there. So many people, whom I had met stateside, were living in the Ivory Coast. I began to date Dr. Kanga with the thought of marriage, as he had proposed to me on my first visit to Abidjan. I soon learned, however, that the two of us didn't match. We parted ways and I lived a beautiful life in Abidjan, Ivory Coast. I became a consultant to Dr. David French, Director of S.H.D.S. (Strengthening Health Delivering Systems). The program was funded by the United States Agency of International Development (US/AID) and The University of Boston, Massachusetts. I learned so much. I worked with the Ivorian and American Government in delivering the programs of S.H.D.S. I met people who came from everywhere, so many different cultures. The majority of persons in The Ivory Coast were exceptionally kind to me. Dr. David French's wife was a sister to Simeon Booker, D.C. Bureau Chief of Jet magazine. I lived with Dr. French, his wife and family for a period of time, before I found an apartment which was shared with me by a sister from Martinique. A lovely sister, who worked for the Arthur Anderson accounting firm.

I enrolled in the University of the Ivory Coast to study French. The student I.D. enabled me to travel into any African country at a 50% discount. I took advantage of that and traveled often to many countries in West Africa. There was always someone in those African Countries to look after me. I was never a stranger, and was always afforded the best of care. What a blessing.

One weekend while living in the Ivory Coast, a friend and I visited a leper colony. People suffering with leprosy, some so severely damaged from the disease, their faces looked like half a person. I was told to avoid those who were heavily stricken with leprosy. I did not adhere to that advice. Instead, I hugged many of the leprosy patients. I talked with them, many had difficulty in speaking, and prayed with them. A Catholic mass service was held and many diplomats and others attended. It was a very interesting and emotional visit. The director of the colony said that he rarely had a visitor to respond the way I did, who without hesitation met and greeted the lepers. I thought how blessed me and my family are after seeing not only the leper colony, but to see so many suffering men, women, and children in the villages I visited in Africa.

I had the pleasure to meet the leader of The Ivory Coast, President Felix Houphonet-Boigny, his wife and family members. I had the privilege to visit the First Lady. One of the President's family members by marriage, the Soumah family looked after me. To date, we continue to stay in touch. After a year and a half, living in Abidjan, I thought it best to return to the States. Just prior to my return to the States, I traveled to Guinea, West Africa, to visit my spiritual brother Kwame Toure, also known as Stokely Carmichael. He had since remarried a young woman from Guinea. His first wife Marian Makeeba was also living in Guinea. I also visited her. She is a wonderful woman, who is living in South Africa. Years later, we saw each other again during a visit to South Africa I took with Minister Farrakhan and his delegation. She and Kwame Toure remained on friendly terms. Kwame Toure took me to visit President Se`Kou Toure`. He was a remarkable man, who was strong and stood up for Africa and its people.

Academic Adventure

After returning to the U.S., I decided to return to college. I entered American University whereby I earned a Bachelor of Arts degree in International Relations and Third World Studies. I received a fellowship to John Hopkins School of International Law. In the first semester at John Hopkins, I heard one of my professors say while giving a lecture, something about the "Negro" Kings of Africa. I questioned him and asked, "Why would you say 'Negro' Kings, when in Africa the word 'Negro' is not used?" The professor told me that African people were Negroes. I got up out of my chair, went to the dean and told him the professor was a racist, and that I couldn't continue with my classes. The dean told me not to quit. He said very few Blacks get a fellowship to John Hopkins and that I should remain. I told him that I really needed a rest. I had gotten my degree from American University taking eighteen credits a semester, going from one semester to the next, including summer school as well. I had also traveled to Geneva, Switzerland to study at the University in Geneva, and took an open course study at the United Nations. I could not sit and listen to a racist professor and take the insults. The dean told me to take the leave, and if and when I decided to return, my fellowship would be available.

In my memories, I recall while studying in Geneva, Switzerland, having dinner with a friend who worked at the American Embassy. At the same restaurant sat Chairman Arafat, Leader of the Palestinians. As my friend and I were leaving, we passed his table. I hesitated and asked the waiter, who was nearby, if I could greet Chairman Arafat. I received permission to approach him. I told the people at the table, that it was an honor to greet Chairman Arafat, and although, I was not a Moslem, I wanted to give him the greetings of "As-Salaam-Alaikum." Chairman Arafat looked at me with a warm smile, and told me (in English), that I should never say I'm not a Moslem, because I am, and that one day I would be practicing Islam. I thanked him. I felt a lot of high energy from that experience. I thought to myself, "I am a devout Catholic, and although, I respected my Moslem friends, I would not become a Moslem." Little did I know what God had in store for me. That was in the summer of 1982. In 1983, I met the Honorable Minister Louis Farrakhan, and in 1988, I became a registered Muslim, under his leadership. Chairman Arafat was 100% correct.

What If...

Thinking back to my first trip to Liberia, West Africa, I would often smile to myself and wonder, "What if?" What if, when my friend, A.B. Tolbert, said to me, "My sister, you are on a spiritual path. I can see the spirit of our ancestors all over you. I have someone for you to meet who is also spiritual. I will take you to his village." I looked at him and thought, "Okay, who could he know that is so spiritual?" He told me of a Prince Asiel Ben Israel. He was the Ambassador of The Black Hebrews. I asked A.B., why did you use the word "Black" when you are referring to your African brothers and sisters. He told me the Hebrews were brothers and sisters from America, and the word, "Black" is used in America. He said that his father, President Tolbert, had given these brothers and sisters a village to live and care for themselves. I was interested, because I had studied the Ascended Masters' Teachings with Elizabeth Clare Prophet, and a new form of spirituality was a challenge for me. A.B. then told me that these brothers and sisters are vegetarians, and that they keep the law of God as taught by Moses of the Old Testament. I was all ready to go and meet Prince Asiel and the group of men and women who had come from America to live in Africa. A.B. said, but there is one thing, the men can have as many as seven wives. I stopped in my tracks and said, "What did you say?" A.B. repeated himself, and then added, you know they are something like a cult. I thought, "Well, perhaps I should first meet Prince Asiel before visiting their village." I told A.B. that I would rather wait and meet Prince Asiel.

A.B. Tolbert and his wife hosted a reception at their home. He and Daisy, wanted me to meet their friends and other family members. They invited Prince Asiel, as well as Congressman Yvonne Braithwaite-Burke's husband, who was in Liberia on business. I and the great Prince Asiel met. We became two kindred spirits. He wanted me to visit their village, but time didn't permit because I was scheduled to return for the States within a couple of days.

Seven years after I met Prince Asiel in Liberia, I was blessed to walk in the Holy Land with he and his family. I was so inspired with the Hebrew Community, so much so that I sat and wrote a letter to all my family and friends. The letter I have to this day which I am sharing with you (see appendix pages 151-153). I was warmly received by their Spiritual Leader, The Honorable Ben Ammi Ben Israel, who along with his wives and family, received me as family. I continue to visit Israel, where I am always received with much love and affection. I love my Hebrew family, and they love and care for me. What if? What if I had gone to their village seven years prior in Liberia? It's all in Divine Order!

Once back in the States, Prince Asiel and I truly became brother and sister. I assisted him in terms of setting up meetings and doing P.R. for him and his Nation. Some years later, Prince Asiel was charged with a crime, found guilty and was sentenced to jail. I was there at his trial everyday. I visited him day in and day out while he was in jail. I arranged for him and those with him to hold their Sabbath services in jail, as well as making sure their diet was adhered to by arranging for the Hebrew Chefs to bring their vegetarian meals to them daily, and get paid for their services by the Government.

The Elevator

D uring his trial court hearings, one day, feeling very tired, I said to myself that I was not going to go to the D.C. Courthouse, where Prince Asiel's trial was being held. "I'm sick of going to their trial everyday, I'm not going today." This was my thinking. The Spirit of God, threw me out of bed. I had a duty and was found getting lazy and not servicing my brothers. I knew that God would be displeased with me if I continued with such a negative attitude. "Get behind me Satan." I then hurried, got dressed and "flew" to the courthouse. When I arrived, there were two marshals with one of the jurors, walking toward the elevators. The marshals were verbally beating up on the juror. Once they saw and recognized me from the daily court proceedings, they didn't even want to get on the same elevator as me, because they were wrong in what they were doing with the juror. I stayed with the juror and marshals, and got on the elevator with them. I followed them off the elevator to the room where the jurors were taken.

In the courtroom, the judge asked where had the juror been because he had disappeared from the court. Another court official, other than the two marshals, whom I had seen with the juror, said the juror had turned himself in to him. I immediately sent word to the defense attorney to say that was not true. I was asked by the defense attorney if I would testify as to what I had witnessed. After I was assigned a court appointed attorney, and gave my testimony as to what I saw and heard with and between the juror and the two marshals, my testimony later assisted Prince Asiel and those accused with him to have their case "over turned." They eventually walked out of prison as free Brothers and a free Sister. Giving the testimony was easy, because "truth" will prevail. However, the threats I received and how the enemy tried to paint me on the witness stand (even in the press), caused me much stress and anxiety.

During the time Prince Asiel and those with him were in jail, with the Blessings of God, I, with the help of a pastor from

D.C., arranged for the Honorable Minister Louis Farrakhan to have a meeting in the jail with Prince Asiel and those with him, including a Hebrew sister. That was historical. They met long beyond the hour that had been permitted. It was a high and holy meeting.

Rescue Mission

While living in Abidjan, Ivory Coast, I would oft-times receive a visit from my brother and friend, A.B. Tolbert. On one of his visits, he introduced me to a Dutchman, John Deuss. He was a wealthy businessman who had homes in Europe, Bermuda, New York City, and Wyoming. He took a liking to me and helped me financially when I decided to return to college. He had been the best man at A.B. Tolbert and Daisy's wedding in Liberia. Not long after I returned from the Ivory Coast back to the States, there was a coup in Liberia. President Tolbert had been killed, his wife, it was told, had been beaten, raped repeatedly, and was in prison. President Doe who had been a military man in the Liberian Army, it was said, killed President Tolbert. The President of The Ivory Coast sent a military plane to get his goddaughter, Daisy, and had her flown to the Ivory Coast, where she remained and raised her and A.B.'s two children. I communicated to Daisy in the Ivory Coast, contacted John Deuss in New York, and arranged for him to get monies to Daisy in support of she and her children. He was the God-father to she and A.B.'s daughter. A.B. Tolbert was in prison. John Deuss arranged for me to meet a White man in Washington, D.C. The man had connections with government agents. They wanted me to take hundreds of thousands of dollars to the border of Liberia. I would be met by soldiers who would escort me into Liberia and arrange to get me to the prison. Once there, I would pay large sums of money to the soldiers and get A.B. Tolbert back across the border, where a plane would take him out of the Continent. Fearing nothing and no one but the God I served, I agreed to do it. I fasted and prayed for three days, and the spirit of my ancestors told me to call Elizabeth Clare Prophet, Spiritual Leader of The Church Universal and Triumph, where I had formerly studied. Elizabeth Clare Prophet had met A.B. Tolbert while I was studying with her in Pasadena, California.

Elizabeth Clare Prophet is difficult to reach by phone. She rarely talks via telephone, almost never. But when I placed a call to her, she immediately came to the phone. I shared with her the plight of Liberia, explaining the coup, the situation in terms of President Tolbert being killed, his wife being tortured and raped, and the fact that A.B. Tolbert was in prison about to be killed. I told her that I was ready to go to Africa and do what was necessary to get A.B. freed. I shared with her of the European man whom John Deuss had arranged for me to meet, and the amount of money that was involved.

Elizabeth Clare Prophet was very quiet and, for a few minutes, said nothing. Finally, she said that it was noble of me to take a risk to save my brother's life, but if I went my brother's life would not be saved and neither would mine. She said, "Claudette, stay out of Africa for the time being. Goodbye." That was my answer. I then called off the trip to Liberia. Some months later I learned that A.B. Tolbert was buried alive. I got word from one of the Liberian soldiers who was present that A.B. Tolbert was "Decreeing" as he was being buried. "Decreeing" is a form of prayer taught to students of the Ascended Masters' Teachings.

A New Birth

After I decided not to continue in my graduate studies at John Hopkins University, I prepared myself for travel to Los Angeles, California. My brother and friend, Kwame Toure was in D.C. He and his wife Maryluatou, invited me to attend an embassy reception at the home of the Ambassador of Nigeria, honoring Secretary of State, George Schultz. In route to the ambassador's home, Kwame asked me to get some African music on the radio. I was sitting in the front seat because in the African tradition, even though Kwame's wife was in the car, I was the elder, hence, I sat in front. As I was turning the station, there was a clear and distinct voice, one I put to a picture which I had seen some years ago when Wauneta Lonewolf had shown me pictures of her wedding. I said at that time to Wauneta, "I feel as though I know this man. As I looked at his picture, there is something I see that is special about him." As I looked at his picture, Wauneta not understanding the depth of what I was saying, replied, "Alright now, he is married with nine children." I told her it wasn't like that. The man in the photograph was The Honorable Minister Louis Farrakhan.

Listening to the voice on the radio, I heard Kwame say, "Leave the dial there, that is Minister Farrakhan." I asked, "Who is Farrakhan?" I told Kwame Toure that there was something to his voice that made me feel I already knew him. Kwame said to me "That is the Muslim leader." He told me that I had to meet him, and that he would arrange for the two of us to meet. He said, "That is a must!"

My sister, Patricia Edwards, was working for Marla Gibbs, the actress in Los Angeles, California. She also had a boutique. With both her job with Ms. Gibbs and running the boutique, her work load was heavy. She asked me to come out to Los Angeles and help her with the boutique. I was still studying with Elizabeth Clare Prophet. I also remained loyal to my Catholic teaching. I had studied with the Catholic Nuns from the ages of twelve to fifteen. I had witnessed my maternal grandmother say the rosary everyday at 6:00 p.m. without fail. My grandmother was reared and married in the Catholic Church. Once divorced, she was ex-communicated from the Church. When I was twelve years of age, she took me to a Catholic Church for mass. I then began to study Catholicism. My mother would not let me become Catholic, until finally one day a Priest told my mother, "She is now fifteen and has studied faithfully for three years, allow her to decide on how she wants to worship God." Soon after, I became Catholic.

While in Los Angeles, after going on a retreat with Elizabeth Clare Prophet and the Saints (members are called Saints), I was relaxing at my sister's home reading my Bible. There was a knock at the front door. It was a brother who had become a member of The Nation of Islam. He provided security at Marla Gibbs' Supper Club. He told me that each time he came for my sister, there I would be reading the Bible. He asked me if I had heard of the Holy Qur'an. I told him I read the Qur'an everyday when I lived in the Ivory Coast. An African Moslem brother had given a Qur'an to me prior to the first trip I took to Africa. The brother gave me a <u>Final Call</u> newspaper and told me that Minister Farrakhan would be in Los Angeles the following Sunday, at Ward A.M.E., Church. I told the brother that two of my friends, Kwame Toure and Wauneta Lonewolf, were acquainted with Minister Farrakhan. The brother smiled, and said both persons were friends of Minister Farrakhan.

I began to get a little excited. I had been on a spiritual journey for a long time in "search" of what is the unknown. Perhaps I could better describe the unknown as "completion." Would there ever be "completion" in my life? God had blessed me in so many ways. Most importantly, He had given me good health and had always provided a way for me to financially sustain my lifestyle and that of my son. I was grateful, but for some reason I just didn't feel "complete."

At Ward A.M.E. Church, on a Sunday morning in January of 1983, my sister Patricia and I walked into the church. The pastor of the church was Reverend Frank Reid. I was dressed in all white. As my sister and I entered the church, I gave the Islamic greetings of "As-Salaam-Alaikum." The brother and sister at the door were Minister Khallid Muhammad and his wife. They looked at each other as if to say, "Who is this sister dressed in white and giving us quite clearly the 'greetings'?" My sister and I were taken to the first pew in the upper balcony of the church. Minister Farrakhan came to the podium. He looked like a shining star. His words were so profound and timely. As he spoke, I asked my sister, "Who is that man standing behind Minister Farrakhan, over his right shoulder." Patricia said that it was one of the twins both of whom were F.O.I. (Fruit of Islam is what the Brothers in the Nation of Islam are called), I said, "No, not the twins, but the man with the fez." Then I realized my sister wasn't seeing who and what I saw. I began to hear Minister Farrakhan's voice in a distance, and the man wearing the fez was speaking to me telepathically. What was said to me perhaps should not be shared in this writing. Only once prior, I had such an experience as an out-of-the body spiritual journey.

The next day, my sister received a phone call from Minister Khallid for the two of us to come and visit Mosque #27. Minister Farrakhan was scheduled to speak. We both rushed to the Mosque. At the end of the lecture, Minister Farrakhan invited the guests to come up and greet him. I went up, told the Minister I had a message for him. He pointed to Minister Khallid and told me to go and put what I had to say in writing and give it to Minister Khallid who would give it to him. I went and wrote a lengthy letter, telling Minister Farrakhan that I was on a spiritual journey. I went on and on. Finally, I ended my letter and gave it to Minister Khallid. Once back at my sister's home, I sat up until the early morning. My sister came into my room and asked me why hadn't I gone to bed. I told her that I was waiting for Minister Farrakhan to call. My sister said to me, "Girl, you must be crazy, Minister Farrakhan is not going to call you, why should he?" I told my sister that I had put in my letter that I would expect a call from him. My sister told me, "Get some sleep. You sound crazy."

The next day, my sister and I received a call from the Secretary of the Mosque, inviting us to Oakland, California; Minister

Farrakhan would be speaking there the next day. My sister and I, rushed to the airport for a flight from Los Angeles to San Francisco. All flights to Oakland, California were sold out. After landing in San Francisco, my sister and I hailed a taxicab for Oakland. The cab driver asked "Where to ladies?" Both of us looked at each other with a question mark on our face. Neither of us had brought the address where the Minister was scheduled to speak. The taxi driver was getting impatient. He needed an address. We were reluctant to give the taxi driver Minister Farrakhan's name, because neither of us knew what he may have said against the Minister or Islam. Finally, I told him that we were going to hear a lecture by Minister Farrakhan, the Islamic Leader, but we didn't have the address of the venue. The taxi driver smiled and said, "As-Salaam-Alaikum, sisters. I will take you where you need to go." What a blessing. After the lecture, my sister and I were invited backstage to have words personally with the Minister. We both were quite nervous. When approaching the Minister, who seemed quite calm and at peace, he greeted us and asked if we had ever attended a "Saviours' Day"? We both said we had not. Minister Farrakhan briefly explained "Saviours' Day" and asked us if we would like to attend. He told us that the Nation of Islam would provide our travel expenses as well as hotel. Being independent, I said that we could defray our own travel expense. He told us that we would be his guests and our hotel cost would be taken care of by the Nation. I then asked him if he had received my letter. He told me that he had, and much of what I wrote was quite interesting. Without thinking, I told him that I had waited up all night for him to call. My sister then told the Minister that she had told me, "Go to bed, the Minister is not going to call you." Minister Farrakhan said, "If she had put a phone number in the letter for me to reach her, I would have called." I almost fell out of my chair. How could I have not put my phone number in the letter?

A month later, arriving in Gary, Indiana, my sister and I attended our very first "Saviours' Day." In attendance were Kwame Toure and Prince Asiel Ben Israel. I was so pleased to see both of my spiritual brothers in attendance which helped to make me feel

I was in the right place at the right time. Minister Farrakhan, his wife, Mother Khadijah, their family and staff were all quite kind to my sister and me. They made us feel very comfortable. My sister and I also met Minister Farrakhan's mother. She reminded me of my paternal great-grandmother, who was also quite frank when she spoke.

The Far East

Later in the year of 1983, I had an opportunity for travel to the East (China, Japan and the Philippines), with a group of eighteen persons who were in the marketing and travel business. The delegation was made up of Whites with the exception of myself and one other Black person who didn't look Black, but instead like an Asian person. While in Japan (the first stop on our tour), I was visited by the Ambassador to Japan from Guinea. He was the nephew of President Se`kou Touré of Guinea. I had contacted President Toure` through friends in Washington, D.C., and through my brother and friend, Kwame Toure. The President had sent word to his Ambassadors to look after me in Japan and China. The Ambassadors learned of my arrival date to Japan and my arrival dates to China. Upon our arrival to China, we stayed at the housing complex where President Nixon had stayed when he visited China in 1972, at the invitation of Premier Zhou Enlai. At the time, our delegation was in China (1983), the Chinese had not become "Americanized". The men and women were wearing Maoist uniforms, or the women were wearing long skirts. I was intrigued with China. The Great Wall! I was told by our Chinese guide to walk up the Great Wall to a certain distance and I would be blessed for the rest of my days. The Forbidden City was educational. Simply Beautiful. I, and those with our delegation, left no stone unturned in Beijing. Unlike my second trip to The People's Republic of China (The Women's World Conference in 1995), there had been no students' and workers' march (100,000) where in Tiananmen's Square 5,000 died, and 10,000 were injured at the hands of Army troops, as the result of The Soviet Leader Mikhail Gorbachev's visit to China.

In our tour of China, after leaving Beijing, our delegation journeyed on to Lanzhou, Shanghai, Taiyuan, and Xian, where we visited the 2,200 year old terra-cotta buried army, that had been discovered by farmers who in 1975 were digging for a well. There were some 8,000 figures, all arranged in battle formation guarding the nearby tomb of China's first Emperor, Qin Shi

Huang (221-209 B.C.). Before, it was said an army of men were actually buried alive with their rulers. To date, over 1.5 million tourists visit this site in Xian.

Our delegation visited several more cities in China. We rode the double back camel through the Gobi Desert. What an adventure. Our small aircraft had mechanical trouble. There we were at the border of China and Mongolia in the Gobi Desert. In 1983, America did not have diplomatic relations with Mongolia, hence, it had to be agreed between the Chinese, American and Mongolian Government for our delegation to enter Mongolia and stay there until a plane would come for us. While in Mongolia, the delegation was told they could not go out into the city. I knew that Mongolia had Moslem citizens, so I greeted everyone with a big smile, saying "As-Salaam-Alaikum." A government official came and got me and said that I had the freedom to go into the city. They thought I was Moslem. Off I went, to a movie, shopping and walking and greeting the people. It was nightfall before I returned. Everyone had begun to worry about me, not realizing that, although I was in Mongolia, I was at home and safe.

From China, our delegation traveled back to Japan. After the delegation departed for the U.S., I stayed with Ambassador Toure and his family. I toured many of the major cities of Japan. Mr. Tijari, a Japanese man who befriended the Most Honorable Elijah Muhammad and who was instrumental in assisting with the purchasing of whiting fish for marketing by the Believers, joined me in Tokyo. We traveled to one of their Spiritual Centers. He introduced me to their management. Their Spiritual Center was comprised of extremely wealthy Japanese men and women who gave back a portion of their wealth to operate the Spiritual Center which provided many of the basic needs for the poor.

Mr. Tijari was a kind man, up in age, but who moved swiftly. After returning to the States, I arranged for him to meet my Hebrew family. He, in turn, made preparations for a few of the Hebrew members to travel and meet persons in Japan who would further train them with the art of tofu dishes. He assisted in their purchasing of tofu machines that produce all kinds of tofu products. After Mr. Tijari visited the Hebrew community in Dimona,

Israel, he arranged for a member of the Hebrew community to live and be trained in Japan for the processing of tofu products. To date, in Dimona, the Hebrews operate a highly successful tofu factory, distributing tofu products throughout Israel.

While in Japan, I visited the Grand Buddha. It is said that once a person circles the Grand Buddha seven times, touch the Buddha upon completion of circling, then say a prayer, they will be truly blessed with their prayers being answered within seven years.

I traveled throughout Japan by car and train. I went to Yokohama, Kyoto, Osaka, into the mountain region, and Hiroshima. The people of Japan were so friendly and kind to me. I learned much from the Japanese who I found to be quite intelligent and humble.

Bahia, The Africa of Brazil

O ne of the persons I met in Japan was Ambassador Cisse and his wife, Madame Cisse. He was the Senegalese Ambassador to Japan. His wife was Brazilian. Later, when I visited Brazil, where they had a home in Rio de Janeiro, they hosted me during my stay. I visited that country as a representative for Councilman Bob Ferrell of Los Angeles, California. The city of Salvador is a sister city to Los Angeles. I met with American Embassy officials and the City Fathers of Salvador to do that which Councilman Bob Ferrell had asked me to do. I presented to the officials, a Proclamation from the Los Angeles City Council stating the relationship between the two cities. In Bahia, where there is a large segment of persons who were brought to Brazil from Nigeria, and who kept their Nigerian Culture, not integrating much with the locals, are more "African" than Africans. It seems that no one else in all the Black slave world fought as hard to keep their customs like the Blacks in Brazil. Bahia is the Black ghetto of Pelourinko in the soul of Brazil, the navel of the universe, one of the most mystical places in the world. Visiting Bahia, in Salvador, in Pelourinko, I could strongly feel the spirit of my ancestors. Salvador, the capital of the state of Bahia, is the third largest city in Brazil. Its population is approximately 3 million people, with about 85 percent of its citizens Black. This is the largest concentration of persons from African descent in the Western Hemisphere. The people are Black with a mixture of Portuguese and other European groups.

The African-based religion Candomblé and Capoeira, brought to Brazil from West Africa, had a High Priestess who was extremely spiritual. She was well-known worldwide. I had been told by the American Consultant that I would not get an opportunity to see her. Well, not taking "no" for an answer, I went to her compound, announced myself and as God Willed it, I visited with the Grand High Priestess. I talked with her, prayed with her, and asked to take a photo. As the spirit would have it, when the film was developed, it was completely blank. The Priestess had told me that she never allowed anyone to take her photo.

The Capoeira of the religion is a dance and self-defense all in one. It is a form of martial arts, which I found to be very beautiful and quite breathtaking. From the many Brazilians I was blessed to meet and converse with, I learned during my stay in Pelourinko which is called the Cidade Alta (Upper City), that this was the city where the slaves were brought to be sold at auctions. Some were sent there by their owners as punishment to be beaten and tortured for infractions no matter how large or small.

When I would hear these stories, I would go to the Church of Our Lady of the Rosary for the Blacks and pray. The energy was so heavy around me. I felt like a magnet receiving the energies from my forefathers. The slavery in Brazil and that within the United States was throughout their colonial stewardship, which lasted until 1832. The Portuguese never stopped bringing captive Africans to Brazil until long after Brazil's 1850 law against slave trade. In America, the importation of slaves was banned in 1807, but in America, the American slaveholders bred Blacks in large numbers. In America, within a single generation, American slaves lost nearly all the languages, customs and cultures brought over from Africa. However, in Brazil the African slaves preserved their languages, customs, and ways of life. In Bahia, there was a large population of African Moslems, who rebelled and kept their culture, and who remain in Bahia to this day. One of the strong African women who fought alongside her male comrades to form the Igreja de Nossa Sambosa do Rosario Dos Pretos (the Catholic Church I visited). There is a statue of her. Her name was Anastasia. She came from African royalty and was sold into slavery. She fought off the slave master, and refused his advances. So the story goes, she was gagged with a metal clamp, and the lead in the metal poisoned her, and she later died. In Bahia, she is considered to be a revolutionary, and in San Paulo and Rio, she is celebrated as a passive martyr. I met with many of the elders in Bahia, and learned so much about my people. Some told me I was a spirit, returning to my homeland. They said some slaves did escape Brazil and ventured on to America on slave ships. I do know that my maternal grandmother's grandfather was Portuguese. His name was Pedro Cardova. He was born in 1847, in New Orleans, Louisiana. According to my grandmother, Mr. Cordova's father came from Brazil, and his mother was Black African and his father came from Portugal.

Many of the people in Bahia speak Yoruba. The children are taught Yoruban for singing and praying in ceremonies. In leaving Bahia, I felt that I had made a connection, a link between Africa-Brazil-America through Candomble. While in Liberdale, the largest Black district in Brazil, I connected with many of my brothers and sisters, some of whom wanted me to discuss with them Malcolm X. Many of our people in the District of Liberdale considered themselves to be revolutionaries. One of their revolutionary warriors, who helped Brazil gain independence from the Portuguese in 1832, was Maria Felipa de Oliveira. The African influence is heavy in Bahia.[1]

Haiti

In one of my many travels, I experienced a very high and spirited meeting with a High Priestess in Haiti. My spiritual cousin Jackie Wooley-Bryant, who has now made her transition, visited her home country with me accompanying her on two different occasions. Our first trip, my son and I traveled to Haiti with Jackie. We toured the island of Haiti, covering much of the island. We saw poor, poor folk. Both visits to Haiti made me really look at the plight of the poor. Countries in Africa with all the diseases and poverty, still did not touch on what I saw in Haiti. Two of Jackie's sons, Karenda and Travis are my godsons.

Marvin Gaye

Years ago, Marvin Gaye was introduced to me by the artist, Ernie Barnes. He and I became close friends. Marvin, at the time, was dating a young woman by the name of Janice. She, Marvin Gaye and her mother spent time in D.C. When Janice was to give birth to their daughter, Nona, who is now a singer and actress, I spent time with the family. Some years later, while living in California, I spoke often to Marvin Gaye's mom, who told me not to try and visit her son. She said, "Claudette, you won't know him now." Just prior to my leaving Los Angeles for Israel at the end of March in 1984, I went to Marvin Gaye's home, walked up the steps, but something stopped me as I was about to knock on the door. That was late in the evening. I turned around, got back in my car and drove away. The next day, I departed the States for Israel. Landing in Israel, I heard the sad news that Marvin Gaye had been shot and killed by his own father, a very sad moment indeed. I called Janice from Israel. I wanted Janice to contact Prince Asiel and come to Israel. I knew that being in Israel with the Hebrew brothers and sisters would lift Janice's spirit. I later learned that Janice and Prince Asiel spoke, but to my knowledge, Janice did not visit Dimona.

Continuing on the Journey

Ibegan to assist the Believers in the Nation of Islam with Public Relations and Protocol. I would travel to cities where Minister Farrakhan was scheduled to speak, oft-times bringing as many as twelve to fifteen of my friends. I became quite comfortable working on a volunteer basis with the Believers. In 1984, Minister Farrakhan asked me to assist him with the Nation of Islam's first International "Saviours' Day." It was quite a learning experience for me. I came to Chicago, lived with the Hebrews and worked with Minister Farrakhan and his staff. The "Saviours' Day" was very successful. Colonel Muammar Qaddafi was the guest speaker via satellite.

Once I returned to Los Angeles from Chicago, after working with the Honorable Minister Louis Farrakhan at their first International "Saviours' Day" Convention, I stayed in Los Angeles, and then traveled back to D.C. I was then approached by a dear friend, Curtis McClinton, who was the Deputy Mayor of Economic Development in Mayor Marion Barry's administration. He wanted me to oversee a special project and take the responsibility to get the job done within a year. The program was called, "The Deputy Mayor of Economics' 'Call Program'." I was to call on the top 100 businesses in the Washington Metropolitan area. I met with the CEO's, presidents and/or vice presidents of corporations, informing them of the monies that were available in the District government to help them develop their corporations, and training programs within the District government, that would provide assistance to their employees. The "Call Program" generated revenue for the District of Columbia, because with the government loans to these 100 corporations, monies were returned to the District government with interest. In addition, the training programs provided by the District government to the corporations, made for an excellent relationship with the officers of the 100 corporations and the Mayor of the District of Columbia.

I took the assignment and excelled to the point that the corporations wanted the deputy mayor to extend the "Call Program" for another six months. During the time I was director of the "Call Program," I was also assisting my Hebrew brothers and a sister who had been sentenced to jail. The deputy mayor called me into his office. He told me that he had seen my name in the paper as a witness in the Hebrew case. He wanted me to stop with the Hebrew case, because it may reflect on my position as his Director of the "Call Program." Before the deputy mayor could finish his sentence, I gave him a "sermon," "How dare you," I said, "to try and deny me from doing God's Will." When I finished with my "sermon," the deputy mayor understood and didn't question me any further. I continued the six months, and continued to assist the Hebrews.

After the eighteen month project with the deputy mayor, I was asked by Mousa (a Palestinian brother), to be vice president of marketing for his travel agency, "Manara". I had met him at the 1983 "Saviours' Day" in Gary, Indiana. I befriended him, and to the objection of some of my friends, took the position at his travel agency, whereby I often did over $20,000 to $25,000 a week in sales. Some of my friends and some family members objected because of Mousa's connection with Libya. I was told by one of my political friends that the travel agency was owned by the Libyan government. That didn't stop me, because as far as I knew, Mousa was the owner. He had been kind to me. He introduced me to many of his Palestinian and Libyan friends and family members, all of whom had been nice and from what I could see, were of no threat to the American government.

I enjoyed my tenure at Manara. Congressman Jack Kemp (R-N.Y.), was running for the Republican nomination for the Presidential Election. I was blessed to secure a contract with his Campaign Headquarters staff, several of the Washington Redskin players, and many of the U.S. Congressmen's travel. "I was rolling", so to speak. Manara Travel Agency received the contract to arrange travel for over 100 persons (400 in total from many countries including the United States), who at the invitation of Colonel Muammar Qadhafi, President of Libya, were invited to witness damage of the bombing that had taken place in Libya which destroyed his home, killing his adopted baby daughter. The bombings were done (it is said) by the American government.

The Truth Revealed

One of my biological sisters, a friend who was a reporter with the <u>Washington Afro</u> newspaper, a Hebrew brother, and I took the journey. We departed from New York, stopped in Malta overnight, and journeyed on to Libya. We were well received. So much rich history in Libya. The Libyan Government hosted all 400 persons royally. There were some difficulties, because some of the guests acted other than themselves. It was said that several persons (from Canada and England) were killed on the tour because they went far beyond being guests of the Libyan government. With my close ties to Liberia, I was invited to the Liberian Ambassador's home for dinner. I received approval from my Libyan host to visit the residence of the Liberian Ambassador. During my visit, the ambassador took me, my sister and our friend on the rooftop of his residence. He showed us where the Ambassador of France and the Ambassador of Switzerland, as well as the Ambassador of the U.S., lived. Their residences were all in the radius of the Ambassador of Liberia's home. He told us that he and many of the other ambassadors had received a warning from the American government that something was about to happen in Libya whereby they and their families and staff should leave immediately from Libya.

The Liberian Ambassador told us that, although, many of his fellow colleagues in the diplomatic corps did take the warning and had left the country, that he remained in Libya. He said that he placed a call to Muammar Qaddafi to let him know of the warning the ambassadors had received, and to also let Colonel Qaddafi know that he was remaining in Libya, but had sent his wife and children out of the country.

The ambassador shared with me and those with me, that the night of the bombings he went on his roof, just where we were standing, and he saw the American Fighter Jets fly over the area of Muammar Qaddafi's home and dropped bombs. He said it was the intended target of the bombing. I thanked the ambassador. I told him that he was a very loyal and brave person to have stayed even after receiving the warning from the American Embassy. His residence had not been damaged, but a few of the other ambassador's residences that were near, Colonel Muammar Qaddafi's residence had been damaged by the bombings. My sister, our friend and I returned to the housing compound where all of the 400 guests were staying. The ambassador's words had somewhat shaken us. He saw first hand what had happened, and to know that, in fact, the American government had done such an evil act really upset me. I told my sister and our friend not to discuss what the Liberian Ambassador had told us. We all agreed not to discuss with any of the persons on the tour what they had heard. Once we returned to the U.S., I told them they could do what they wanted.

Mrs. Qaddafi and two of her older children, along with Libyan officials had a ceremony for the 400 guests at their residence that had been bombed. All of the guests were taken through the wreckage of the home. It was devastating to see the ruins of their home as a result of the bombings. Lined up like an art exhibit were paintings that children had drawn paintings depicting what they thought of the Americans who had flown the planes and did such a horrific act. I took pictures of everything I saw. The reporter from the <u>Washington Afro</u> newspaper filmed everything.

The trip to Libya was historical. It hit the media worldwide of the 400 persons from the U.S., Canada, Germany, and England who were on the tour. When I and those with me departed Libya, we went to Malta. Our Hebrew brother did not stay in Malta with us, he and the delegation traveled back to the U.S. My sister, our friend and I stayed in Malta where we toured and shopped. All the gifts we had received in Libya, and all our filming, we mailed via express back to the States from Malta, just by chance they would lose our luggage. Those items and pictures were too priceless to lose. I had gotten word while we were in Malta, that the American government had a list of all the Americans who had visited Libya, and once they entered the U.S., all the gifts and film from Libya was taken from them. Thank God that I, and those with me, had the foresight to mail all our gifts and film ahead of us. I had called one of my Congressmen friends to ask if I could send our gifts and film to his office to be assured nothing was taken or damaged. He complied. From Malta, my sister, our friend and I went to Rome, Italy. My sister became ill and had to return to the States. She went through U.S. Customs without any trouble. My friend and I toured Rome and had a wonderful visit. We toured the Holy See (the Vatican), and visited Germany before returning to the States. We had friends in Germany who looked after us. I visited the mosque in Germany, and met with many of the Moslems in that community. Our visit to Germany was great. Upon returning to the U.S., it was clear sailing, no problems. The American government could not arrest us because we didn't enter Libya with our American passport, we didn't spend the American dollars as we were guests of Libya and had no need of anything, nor did we travel to Libya on an American aircraft. All American aircraft had stopped flying to Libya.

As a second job, I once worked for Turk Thompson, who was a distinguished attorney in Washington, D.C., and became a Senior Superior Court Judge. I learned much from my work with Attorney Thompson. When he became Judge, I remained acquainted with him. Anything about the law I needed to know, I would seek the advice of his associates. I had no fear of traveling to Libya, and had covered all that I needed to know about the law as it applied to me, my sister, and my friend's journey with the American delegation to Libya.

I Fear No Evil

Once back in the States, and months later, a man came to Manara Travel Agency. He asked, "Are you Claudette Marie Johnson," I said, "Yes," and he immediately gave me a subpoena to appear before the grand jury. Mousa and some of his acquaintances were being accused of working with Libya against the U.S. I retained the services of an attorney. In addition, I took counsel with some of my attorney friends and Judges, and went before the grand jury with no fear, because I knew that I had done no wrong. My attorney told me if I got frightened or could not answer any of the persons on the grand jury who would pose questions, I would be allowed to stop and ask for my attorney. At a grand jury hearing, the client is alone with the grand jury. The attorney for the client is not present. At the hearing, I never blinked an eye. I was not frightened by them nor afraid. Some of the questions posed were out of order: questions about the Nation of Islam; questions about my personal life; and questions about Libya and its leader. I told the grand jury that to ask those kinds of questions, I felt, was out of order. What did those questions have to do with what the government was charging Mousa and his friends? I asked to be excused. The questions ended and I was excused. My attorney was quite surprised that I had not called for his assistance during my stand before the grand jury. The devil is the devil. When a person has God with them, that person will always be the winner. This, too, was an experience that showed me how, when the enemy wants to destroy you, they use all kinds of tactics. Mousa left the country and the two other persons went to jail. I visited them in jail. Sometime shortly thereafter, one had been released and the other deported back to his home country. Manara Travel Agency remained in business for a while then was taken over by another travel agency and. I went on about my business and never looked back. I had my attorney to have the grand jury hearing records sealed so as not to be used against me in any way.

The Maori and Aboriginal People

In my travels to New Zealand and Australia, it was like "smooth sailing". I had met June Jackson and her daughter-in-law, while they were visiting The Honorable Minister Louis Farrakhan in Atlanta, Georgia. June Jackson liked an outfit I was wearing. I went to my room, changed my garments and returned to give June Jackson the outfit that she had liked so well on me. I had learned during my stay in Africa, that when a person deeply admires something on you, and if your heart tells you to give it to that person, do so. In New Zealand, I was received by June and her husband Bob. They were terrific hosts. I learned so much about the Maori Culture. I traveled to many cities in New Zealand. I had been told that Master Fard Muhammad, the Founder of the Nation of Islam, had traveled to New Zealand in route to America. I was taken to a family's home that was said to be where Master Fard Muhammad had stayed, and saw a picture that I was told to be him. It looked like Master Fard Muhammad.

In New Zealand, the Maoris are approximately 340,000, with only six of the 120 members of the House of Representatives elected directly by the Maori people. A dear friend, Senator Carole Mosley-Braun, the first Black female elected to the U.S. Senate, who, after her defeat the second term, was appointed by President Bill Clinton as the Ambassador to New Zealand. In our talks, she really enjoyed her tenure as ambassador and that the Maori people treated her well.

From New Zealand, I traveled to Australia. I was received by Dr. Roberta Sykes, one of the first Aboriginal women to receive a Ph.D. from Harvard University. She has since setup a program sending an Aboriginal woman to the university every so many years, to graduate school. Dr. Sykes arranged for my travel to Alice Springs, where many of the Aboriginal people lived. I met a woman from one of the Aboriginal Women's Organization. She introduced me to many of the progressive Aboriginal people, who were working hard for the upliftment of their people. I attended many of their meetings and was invited to speak on a public radio program. I spoke of The Honorable Minister Louis Farrakhan and the work he is doing worldwide. There were many call-ins, all with positive remarks concerning Minister Farrakhan and The Nation of Islam. I mailed an audio tape of the broadcast to the Honorable Minister Louis Farrakhan. I later learned from him, that I should not have gone on the radio without his permission. He said I was in that country, traveling alone. To go on public radio speaking about him and the Nation of Islam, could have caused a security problem for me. A lesson I learned well. I toured Alice Springs. Going into the camps of the Aboriginals, I saw that theywere living in extremely poor conditions. Many of the Aboriginal people I met and spoke with didn't want to mix with the Whites. They wanted their land back and wanted to live according to their culture. Many of the Aboriginals had mixed with the Whites, some with the East Indians. In Australia, overall there are over three million Europeans, half of whom are British, who have entered that country since 1945. With the 50,000 Aborigines, and the 150,000 part-Aborigines, they are mostly "detribalized".

I visited Ayers Rock which is the largest rock in the world. It is quite historical with writings in the caves on the rock with symbols telling the story of the Aborigines. The original peoples of Australia are beautiful and highly spiritual people. Much like the American Indians, they have been given alcohol which has destroyed many of them. Unlike many of the other countries I visited, I saw animals I had never seen before, like the kangaroos, dingos (wild dogs), koalas and strange looking raccoons.

The artwork of the Aborigines is unique, seen in no other country in the world. I was blessed to have been received by the Islamic Imam and his wife of Alice Springs. After listening to me on the radio broadcast, they invited me to their home for dinner, where I met many of the Moslems in their community. They told me stories of how their people had migrated from the East to Australia.

The Great Eagle

My memories are taking me to 1984, while in Los Angeles, California, I learned that Wauneta Lonewolf, my American Indian sister, and her husband were living in Los Angeles. They were staying with Sister Beverly Todd, a beautiful and sensitive actress. One evening, I joined Wauneta, Chief Ernie Longwalker and his wife, Warrior Woman for a "sweat lodge." My first experience in a "sweat lodge" was with Chief Ernie Longwalker, his wife and several other Indian men. As I crawled into the tee-pee, there in the center were burning hot rocks, where water was splashed on the hot rocks by Chief Longwalker causing hot, hot, hot, steam. One could only grasp the sage and other herbs and breathe slowly trying one's best not to faint. In those moments, I reflected back when I was merely a little girl, five years of age, who had been savagely sexually abused by my paternal grandfather, and my paternal great-grandmother had soaked me with these same kinds of herbs. Now I was feeling cleansed. I prayed and asked God to continue in giving me strength to do His Will and to open my eyes so that I may see what He wanted me to see, as I go about doing that which He had in store for me to do. As I prayed, I felt the top of the tee-pee flapping as though someone was on top of the tee-pee hitting it. After all the rounds of prayer and smoking the pipe as it was passed from one participant in the tee-pee to the other, I crawled out of the tee-pee exhausted. Chief Ernie Longwalker told me that I did excellent, because to go in with the Chief and others who had been doing "sweat lodges" for years, I did well. I asked Chief Longwalker and his wife, "Why was there someone hitting the tee-pee at the top?" Chief Longwalker said that, that was not a person, but that was the "great-eagle." He said, "It is a blessing for you." He told me that people rarely sense the "great-eagle." I have taken a total of seven "sweat-lodges" with my American Indian brothers and sisters, always as a result feeling spiritually renewed.

In Search of Another Blessing: The Elephants of Mali

Elephants have always been special to me. I feel that the elephant represents strength and yet tenderness. When I visited Burkina Faso, West Africa, one of the domestics in the house where I was staying told me many stories about the elephants. He told me of the migration of the elephants, and that a person is blessed if they can go to the border of Ghana and Burkina Faso and see the elephants that have migrated down from Mali. He told me elephants can live to be sixty years of age, if the poachers don't kill them.

With the excitement of the possibility of seeing a herd of elephants, my friend and I, with a driver took off about 2:00 a.m. in search of these elephants. We sat at the border for about two hours and then they came. Beautiful elephants. There were female, male and young elephants. The driver told me there were a few male elephants in the group. I got so excited. I ran quickly with my camera, and began to take pictures. The driver ran and got me and explained that I was putting myself in harm's way, because when there are young elephants in the herd, the matriarch protects the young. The older elephants can hear an unfamiliar sound quite easily. He told me, that I was clicking the camera and not walking softly. "The elephants will hear you and charge at you quickly." He said, "Let's get out of here." I wanted to stay and take more pictures of those beautiful animals, but just as I was deciding to stay, one of the larger elephants turned and looked my way. The elephant appeared as though it would charge at me, I hurriedly got back in the car, and we drove off quickly, looking back to take another glance of such beautiful and handsome animals.

Blessings of a Son

As I turn to my memory, remembering all the places God has allowed me to be and all the people God has allowed me to meet, I feel quite blessed. I have been truly blessed to experience the joy of motherhood, to have a son who has been a blessing to me. He really never gave me trouble. I worked hard, sometimes three jobs at a time, to afford our lifestyle and to keep him in schools where he would be well-educated. One day my son came home quite upset. He was about 11 years of age. I asked him why was he so angry and upset. He told me that a boy had called him a Black Nigger. I told my son, "Well, you are not a nigger, but you are Black." He said, "No, I'm not Black. You and grandma are Black, but not me." He had fair skin and his hair, at age 11, was sandy in color. After hearing him say that, I thought, "Here he is attending a lab school at Catholic University where there are mostly White students, and I am not really teaching him 'Blackness' - not in color, but in 'consciousness'." I thought about our conversation and decided that I had better do something or he will grow up not knowing his "Blackness".

I had a friend, Mrs. Olive Raullerson, whose husband Hank was the Director of Peace Corps in Kenya, East Africa. I called them in Kenya and explained what my son had said with reference to his not being "Black," and seeing it only as a color. Arrangements were made, and within two weeks, Tony was off to Kenya, East Africa where he stayed for the entire summer. Upon his return, he knew that he was a young Black brother, afro and all.

MILLION MAN MARCH

1995

MILLION WOMAN MARCH
1997

MILLION FAMILY MARCH

2000

MILLIONS MORE MOVEMENT

2005

MEET ME IN WASHINGTON, DC

THE MILLIONS MORE MOVEMENT

OCT. 15, 2005

From the Church to

the Mosque

B lessings come in so many ways. After two years of assisting Minister Farrakhan and the Believers at Mosque #27 and Mosque #4, one Sunday, I was sitting in the D.C. Mosque hearing a lecture. I heard Minister Dr. Abdul Alim Muhammad say, "All you 'would be' Muslims, with one foot in the door, and one foot out the door – get up and become your own." That did it for me. I wrote my processing letter in 1985 and in 1988, I finally recited the "Lessons," and became a member in the Nation of Islam. The rest is history. The Teachings of The Most Honorable Elijah Muhammad have been good for me. The work that I do for the Nation has helped me to grow. My brothers and sisters in Dimona, Israel have most definitely contributed to my well-being.

One Hand Helps the Other

In 1992, I received a call from Ron Clark, Director of R.A.P. (Regional Addiction Prevention) Incorporated, a substance abuse shelter-program, that I became acquainted with when I met Ron Clark back in the early 1970's. Being acquainted with Ron Clark and actively involved in assisting in some of R.A.P.'s programs, helped me to somewhat have a better understanding of those who were substance abusers. I had a very low tolerance for persons who were users of drugs. Ron wanted me to introduce Zev Putterman to Minister Farrakhan. He was a movie producer and a friend who was also the former husband of Ron's former Jewish wife. I told Minister Farrakhan that there was a Jewish producer who wanted to meet him. I asked the Minister that when he was scheduled to be in California, could the two of them meet? Minister Farrakhan said, no and that he wasn't interested at the time. Then almost a year later, Minister Farrakhan called and asked about the Jewish movie producer. He told me of his upcoming schedule to Los Angeles, and if the person could meet with him in L.A., I was to arrange the meeting. I called Ron Clark and told him all the particulars. The meeting was arranged but I didn't hear anymore about the meeting.

Over the years, my son had become a substance abuser. I had him put out of my D.C. residence, and more or less had little to do with him. He moved to Los Angeles. All I could do was pray for him and work hard thinking that perhaps through my hard work, God would bless me to find an avenue that would drive my son free of the devil.

One evening, I received a phone call. It was Zev Putterman, the movie producer. He told me that he could never thank me enough for arranging the meeting between him and Minister Farrakhan. He then asked, "Are you alright? You sound somewhat sad. If I'm not being too personal, is there something bothering you?" I don't open up to strangers, especially to those I have never personally met. But since Zev had called and told me of his and the Minister's meeting, and some of what they discussed, stating how pleased and happy he was to have met the Minister, I found myself telling Zev Putterman about my son's problems. Zev Putterman asked that I give him my son's phone number. He told me that one of the things Minister Farrakhan recommended to him was that he should join with many of his wealthy friends and reach back and help others. Those were not his exact words, but somewhat his meaning. Zev Putterman told me that he had a Rehabilitation Center in Tucson, Arizona and another in the foothills of California. He said the cost is anywhere from $3,000.00 to $5,000.00 a month. He told me if my son would get to Arizona on his own, he would personally take care of the cost. The only thing Tony had to do was get there and Zev Putterman would take care of the financial matters. He told me that in the Jewish tradition, if someone does good for a person, that person must, in turn, do good for them. "Since you, Claudette did good for me, I will do good for you and take care of your son." Now the problem, so I thought, was getting my son to Tucson, Arizona. Well, there is a God. Tony called one day, and Praise God, he said, "Ma, I'm catching a bus and I'm on my way to Tucson, Arizona." He and Zev Putterman had talked, and if he would get to Arizona, Zev would take care of the rest. My son stayed in that program at Amity for well over a year. After that, Zev Putterman put him in a halfway house and helped him as he entered the University of Arizona, where he graduated a few years later, and now has a sound job, owns a condo, and is a healthy human being, living a righteous and fruitful life. A strong Blackman. All Praise Is Due To Allah (God).

Footprints in the Sand

Ihad been blessed with many brothers and sisters. My father and all three women who gave him children, are deceased. My family, with my son, granddaughter, and great-grandson, are all well and are a joy to me. My granddaughter, in 1995, recited a poem at the Million Man March in front of the U.S. Capitol. The poem was written by Dr. Maya Angelou with words added by Minister Farrakhan. Family is so important. In addition, to all the members of my biological family, I have spiritual sons and daughters and two godsons, all of whom are special to me.

I Have A Dream

Now at the age of sixty-eight, recalling all these memories, perhaps 20 years from now, I may have a collection of more memories, wealthy memories, somewhat like that of the great Dr. Dorothy Height, who I was blessed to meet during the Dr. Martin Luther King, Jr.'s "March on Washington" on August 28, 1963. My dear friend, Mrs. Faye White, who at the time was working for Congressman Charles Vanik (D-OH), and I rode on the bus with the U.S. Congressmen to the March on Washington. We were given permissions by both our employers, neither of whom went to the March. There we were, the only two Congressional staff persons on the bus with nothing but U.S. Senators and Congressmen. We sat near Congressman Gus Hawkins (D-Calif.). The ride back from the 1963 March was most educational because we were privileged to hear the comments of those Congress persons who had attended. Faye and I, at the March, sat near Lena Horne and other dignitaries. We were able to get close enough to meet Dr. Dorothy Height, A. Philip Randolph, and Dr. Martin Luther King, Jr. The Honorable Minister Louis Farrakhan was there standing behind Dr. Dorothy Height; however, I did not know of him at the time. She is very special to me. When I think of Dr. Height, I reflect on success, good health, peace, and joy.

The "Holy" Land

A llah (God) has blessed me to travel and witness the beautiful sites in many Nations of the World. In some of my travels, I have been accompanied by my family members - biological and extended. In some countries I have traveled by myself, and in other countries, I traveled with friends. I was blessed to be in the company of The Honorable Minister Louis Farrakhan and his lovely wife, Mother Khadijah Farrakhan, on several of their World Tours. There has been only one country in all my travels where I was treated badly by its government airport officials, and that was in Israel, where they did all that they could to discourage Blacks from entering Israel because it was believed the sole purpose for Blacks traveling to Israel, was to join the Hebrew Israelite Nation of Dimona.

In my first visit to Israel in 1984 there was no problem, with the exception of my departure from the Israeli Airport. The airport handlers searching my luggage were so rude. They actually took my clothes out of my suitcase and threw some of my clothes on the floor. I had to repack my luggage and, in doing so, missed my return flight back to the States. I had to put my luggage in a holding area, and returned to Dimona. The next day, Councilman Bob Farrell, who was visiting Dimona, escorted me to the American Embassy. I told my story and an Embassy Representative along with the Councilman escorted me to the airport and saw to it that I was properly taken care of and put me on my flight back to the United States. That was an experience in which I was blessed to leave without harm.

My second visit was in January of 1985, after leaving Liberia where I assisted Prince Asiel Ben Israel and Mayor Johnny Ford, with the Black Mayors' Conference. Mayor Ford of Tuskegee, Alabama was the President of the Black Mayors Association. Pastor T.L. Barrett of the Life Center Church of God In Christ Chicago, Illinois, accompanied me from Liberia to Israel, where he and Reverend Dr. Henry Hardy of Cosmopolitan Community Church in Chicago, and others had joined the Black Mayors for their conference, hosted by the Liberian Government.

My third visit in May of 1985, to Israel was terrible. Upon my arrival, the officials at the airport took one look at me, pulled me out of the Customs' line, and escorted me to a room where there were several airport security personnel. They asked me to verify my name. They then accused me of traveling on a "stolen" ticket. They questioned me for about six and a half hours, non-stop. They showed me a mark on my airline ticket which they said indicated it was fake. I told them the ticket had been given to me which I won at a fundraising auction. I knew nothing about the ticket being stolen.

After many hours of questioning, I was taken to a holding room below the airport and detained overnight. I was given no food, and one small glass of water. I had to carry my own luggage, both bags were quite heavy. Once downstairs, I was told to sit on the couch, stay there and someone would come and get me the next morning. Late into the night came two armed male airport officials. I told them in a very stern voice, "If you touch me, you and everyone connected with you will be dead within a year." I then made the sign of the cross with my fingers. The soldiers "flew" back upstairs. Very early the next morning, I was "deported" and sent back to the States via France. Once in France, I called Dimona. I was quite upset and told one of Prince Asiel's wives to let Prince Asiel know that I did not reveal who gave me the airline ticket to the airport authorities. I said that they should find out who had done this to me and why. As much as I had done to help my Hebrew family, I could not understand any Hebrew giving me a stolen ticket to travel. I was quite hurt and upset.

Once I arrived to New York, two F.B.I. agents were waiting for me, as well as two Hebrew brothers. I told the F.B.I. agents unless they had a warrant, I had nothing to say. I then called my son and told him that I would come to Virginia and stay with him at his condo. The Hebrew brothers flew to D.C. from New York with me. We were met in D.C. by two other Hebrew brothers and one Hebrew sister. They escorted me to my son's home, where I stayed for a week before returning to Los Angeles, California.

I later learned from a Hebrew brother, that the brother who was responsible for my airline ticket was banned from their community by The Honorable Ben Ammi. He had indeed given me a "bad" ticket. Many months later, after I had returned to D.C., I was assisting Prince Asiel with his trial as he and others had been charged with criminal activity. Once he and those with him were found guilty, I did all that I could, day-in and day-out, to assist them while they were in jail. The brother responsible for the alleged "bad" ticket, was one of the brothers I was assisting. Until this day, that brother never apologized to me. I did receive an apology from Prince Asiel Ben Israel for what I had gone through. However, I have yet to hear an apology from the brother who allegedly wronged me.

I went to Congressman Mervyn Dymally (D-CA), requesting that he assist me to have the "deportation" removed from my passport record. He could not help me. His staff director never told me why I could not receive assistance from the Congressman's office. I thought to myself, perhaps a White man of high status could get the job done. I went to Congressman Jack Kemp (R-NY), who had later became the Secretary of HUD. Sure enough, Congressman Jack Kemp wrote a letter to the Israelia Ambassador. I sent a copy of the letter to the Secretary of State. Within a month, I received a letter of apology from the Israelia Ambassador, who told me that the doors of Israel would always be open, and that I would never have that kind of trouble again. I thanked The Honorable Jack Kemp and sent a reply thank you letter to the Israelia Ambassador. In all my travels to Israel from then on, I have not encountered any difficulties.

I was on the staff of the Honorable Minister Louis Farrakhan when I was about to take my first trip back to Israel since that 1985 incident. I had my letter of entry from the Israeli Ambassador, my ticket in hand, and Prince Asiel had made all the arrangements. Then early one morning, Minister Farrakhan called and told me that I could not at this time travel to Israel. Without anymore conversation, he was off the telephone. I was quite shaken. I wrote to the Minister from D.C., and sent him a copy of the "apology letter" from the Ambassador of Israel. He still said,

"No." I told Prince Asiel, and he of course asked me "Why?" I didn't know, but I had to do as the Minister said, even though, I nor the Prince Asiel understood the Minister's reason. Months later, almost a year, in a meeting with Minister Farrakhan, he said to me, "Sister Claudette, obedience is better than sacrifice." It didn't dawn on me until weeks later, what he meant. That is one time I was a slow learner.

Since that time in 1985, I have visited Israel approximately 12 times. With each visit, it gets better and better. I have encouraged many of my friends and spiritual family to visit Dimona. Many Believers came, including Mother Tynnetta Muhammad and Minister Abdul Akbar Muhammad during a time when I was also visiting Dimona. I have traveled throughout all of Israel. Each visit is a joy and a learning experience, of which I am forever thankful to God. In my travels to Israel, I have left no stone unturned,. Traveling throughout "The Holy Land" has found me spending time in Mitzpah Ramon, looking from the mountaintop down into the crater, reflecting on the Bible story of Sodom and Gomorrah, where archaeological analysis has discovered the crater is approximately 4 ½ billion years old. Visiting the Dead Sea only a short distance from Mitzpah Ramon was truly a blessing. The Dead Sea, referred to as the "Live Sea" by our Hebrew Brothers and Sisters, cures many ills. To soak in the "Live Sea" makes one feel rejuvenated and much alive.

The city of Arad where the weather is excellent has helped me as an asthma patient. Visiting Arad, one sees and meets many Russian Jews. All through the Negev are beautiful desert land and mountain ranges. Beer Sheva is a fun city with a great bazaar to shop. When I visited Eilat, it is virtually a state within a state. It is a far city from most of the cities in Israel. Very peaceful and quiet, a person can see the Edom Mountains of Jordan from Eilat. I have cruised on the Red Sea from Eilat and saw over into Jordan, toward the Northeast, Egypt toward the South, and Saudi Arabia toward the Southeast. It is breathtaking to see such beauty. I would like to, one day, have a home here because of the picturesque beauty of the land.

Then there is Tiberias in the North of Israel, and also the

Jordan Valley. The history of Tiberias and its surroundings really makes the Holy Books—Bible and Qur'an—come alive. The Sea of Galilee, Massada, the Jordan River, En Gedi, Mt. Tabor, Mt. Carmel, Mt. Hermon, Banais Falls, Mezudaz Nimrod, Sermon on the Mount, Quriyat Shemona, the Golan, Haifa, the Borders of Lebanon and Syria—all upper Galilee. What an experience, so high and holy.

Tiberias is one of the most beautiful cities of Israel, where the Jordan River feeds into the Sea of Galilee and the beautiful mountain ranges, one of which is the Massada. This is the mountain where the Hebrews sought refuge from the Romans for forty years, until finally the Romans reached the top of Mt. Massada. Rather than being captured, the Hebrews (men, women, and children) killed themselves.

Tiberias, which is a part of Galilee in the city whereby Jesus The Christ did much of His ministry, is so richly green with fruits and vegetables growing everywhere. While visiting Tiberias, I often would go and pluck watermelons farmed by the Arabs, who welcomed me.

I have visited Mt. Tabor, the Mountain of Transfiguration, where Jesus, Elijah and Moses met; Mt. Carmel and Mt. Herman. The Banias Falls - simply beautiful. I went down into a carved-out mountain area, where the water flows down into the Jordan River through the mountains and comes out as beautiful waterfalls and springs. Then there is Mezudaz Nimrod which is the Fortress of Nimrod. The Fortress also has an Arabic name, *Kal'at a-Sabiba*, the fortress leaping at its prey.

To go and stand at the place of the Biblical Sermon on the Mount (The Beatitudes), where the Christians have built a church and the area is administered by clergy and nuns, reminded me of my study and practice of Catholicism. It was quite a special experience to be at where Jesus delivered the Sermon on the Mount.

Traveling to the last city north of Israel, Quriyat Shemona, which is on the border of Lebanon and Syria, is truly an experience. I have visited Haifa and Jerusalem, Jericho, Hebron and Jenin on many of my earlier visits to Israel. However, with so much unrest in those cities, I somewhat shy away from visiting because of the political duress and the recent bombings between the Israeli ground forces and Hezbollah of Southern Lebanon in Northern Israel.

Outside of visiting the cities we read about in the Bible all throughout Israel—Bethlehem, Nazareth, Capernaum, Gibeon and all the other cities I've written about, it was quite touching to visit with the Bedouins. The Ishmaelites in Rahat, Israel and Segev, Shalom, Israel. There are over 100,00 Bedouins in Israel, approximately 90,000 in the Negev and 10,000 in the Galilee area.

Many of the Black Arab-Moslem Ishmaelite brothers and sisters are as black as ebony. In the city of Rabat, there are over 240 Moslem communities, of which three are Black communities of Ishmaelites. They are not a part of the West Bank of Gaza, hence, I could visit them, unlike Hebron or Jenin which is restricted.

Visiting Segev Shalom, the African village not too far from Beersheba, is very interesting. It reminded me of a village in West Africa. Segev Shalom is a city of Bedouins. Visiting our Bedouin Ishmaelites is always one of the highlights of my visit to Israel.

The sadness, for me, is seeing our Ethiopian brothers and sisters, who have migrated to Israel but yet do not socialize with the Black brothers and sisters of the Bedouins, nor do they have a rapport with our Hebrew brothers and sisters. Many of the Ethiopians, as it appears, seemed to have lost much of their cultural heritage and connection to African people that are in Israel.

A Nation Within a Nation

My 23 years of being acquainted with the Honorable Minister Louis Farrakhan have been remarkable. My 18 years of practicing Islam and assisting him in the work that Allah Has Ordained him to do has been a Blessing from Allah. The work for Freedom, Justice and Equality for our people has brought me much peace, and has allowed me to learn from such a diversity of folk from all walks of life. People in "high places" from across the globe to the "little people" from places I once would not go.

I've experienced much in terms of how people of political and religious differences can allow themselves to be so divided. I have worked with and for persons from various professional backgrounds, which has given me an insight enabling me to be a helper to Minister Farrakhan.

I was appointed in August of 2005 by Governor Rod R. Blagojevich to serve as a Commissioner on the *Governor's Commission on Discrimination and Hate Crimes*. In the commission meetings, all commissioners were apprised of my being Muslim, who serves under the direction of the Honorable Minister Louis Farrakhan.

The Nation of Islam holds its annual "Saviours' Day" in February of each year. I invite many people to "Saviours' Day", where Minister Farrakhan delivers his keynote address. I invited the commissioners through the chairman, Reverend Willie T. Barrow. The letter was sent to the executive director, Mrs. Kimberly White. She, the assistant director, and several other commissioners attended, none of whom said they were insulted by Minister Farrakhan's words.

There were certain Jewish persons who felt the Minister's words were anti-Semitic and anti-Gay. The news media had an article in the newspapers and much was said on television and in the news for almost ten days straight. I was "attacked", because it was said by some that I should condemn Minister Farrakhan and the governor should remove me from the commission. It went on and on. The governor was reported as saying that he didn't know that I was a member of the Nation of Islam and that he didn't even know who I was. Even in the midst of all the controversy, God Allowed me to be strong and take a "stand". Why attack me? My response to all those attacking me and Minister Farrakhan is to prove him to be wrong. Have an open dialogue with him and prove him wrong. He has said, "Prove me wrong, and I will apologize." And so it is!

"Memories" are my thoughts, reflecting on the many wonderful people I have met, and the places in the world that I have been blessed to visit. Life is a journey full of "Memories." I have shared my "Memories" so that others who have fallen in harm's way, and who have been beaten by society, will know there is a God. All any of us have to do is put our hand in His Hand and humbly ask Him to Guide us on our way. Nothing or no one should prevent us from enjoying the fruits of life. Everyday should be the "beginning" of the rest of our lives. We should live each day to the fullest in a righteous manner; always giving of ourselves to help others.

Thank you for reading my "Memories." I pray that everyone who reads "Memories" will be refreshed and will somehow, no matter how large or how small, benefit from the lessons of my life.

God Bless You.

Countries Visited

I am sharing a listing of countries I have been blessed to visit. God Willing, I plan to some day travel the entire world. These countries are just the beginning of my World Journey, that will cause for my "Memories" to last for a lifetime.

1.   Australia – S.E. Asia
2.   The Bahamas – Caribbean
3.   Barbados – Caribbean
4.   Belgium – Europe
5.   Belize – South America
6.   Benin – West Africa
7.   Botswana – South Africa
8.   Brazil – South America
9.   Burkina Faso – West Africa
10.   Canada – North America
      - Ontario
      - Quebec

11.   Republic of Cape Verde – West Africa
12.   China – East Asia
13.   Congo – Central Africa
14.   Cote d' Ivoire – West Africa
15.   Cuba – Caribbean
16.   Egypt – N.E. Africa
17.   El Salvador – Central America
18.   France – Europe
19.   Gabon – Central Africa
20.   The Gambia – West Africa
21.   Germany – Europe
22.   Ghana – West Africa
23.   Guatemala – Central America
24.   Guinea – West Africa
25.   Guyana – South America
26.   Haiti – Caribbean
27.   Iran – Middle East
28.   Israel – Middle East

29. Italy – Europe
30. Japan – East Asia
31. Jordan – Middle East
32. Liberia – West Africa
33. Libya – North Africa
34. Malaysia – S. E. Asia
35. Malta – Mediterranean
36. Mexico – South America
37. Mongolia – East Central Asia
38. Netherlands – Europe
39. New Zealand – S.W. Pacific
40. Nicaragua – South America
41. Nigeria – West Africa
42. Philippines – S.E. Asia
43. Saudi Arabia – Middle East
44. Senegal – West Africa
45. Sierre Leone – West Africa
46. South Africa – Southern Africa
47. Spain – Europe
48. Sudan – East Africa
49. Suriname – South America
50. Switzerland – Europe
51. Syria – Middle East
52. Togo – West Africa
53. Trinidad and Tobago – Caribbean
54. Tunisia – North Africa
55. Turkey – Asia and Europe
56. United Arab Emirates – Middle East
57. United Kingdom – Europe
58. Virgin Islands – U.S. Territory
59. Puerto Rico – U.S. Territory
60. United States
    - All 50 states
    - District of Columbia
61. Vatican City (The Holy See)
62. Venezuela – Central America
63. Zambia – Central Africa
64. Zimbabwe – South Africa

Dead to The Old Life,
Yielding The New Life of God

Family Tree

Sister Claudette Marie Muhammad
Born – Houston, Texas
02-13-38

Parents:	Travis Johnson II
	Ernestine Edith Henderson
Son:	Anthony L. Pinkins
High School:	Kearny High School
	Graduate June – 1956
	San Diego, California
College:	San Diego Junior College
	University of Southern California
	American University
	Johns Hopkins School of International Law
	University of Abidjan, Coté d' Ivoire, West Africa
	University of Geneva, Switzerland
Siblings:	Margurite Ann Johnson-Wilkens (Deceased)
	Travis Johnson III
	Patricia Belle Johnson-Baker-Edwards
	Rixner Eugene Johnson
	Linda Joyce Johnson-Perkins-Walker
	Faye Ernestine Johnson
	Kathleen Jordan
	James Johnson
	Kenneth Johnson
	Doyle Johnson
	Michael Johnson
	Cheryl Lynn Collier
	Dinetta Gale Rose
	Dwight Johnson

Maternal

Mother: Ernestine Edith Henderson
Born – Houston, Texas / 12-1-19

Grandmother: Margurite Rixner
Born – Galveston, Texas / 6-11-1902

Grandfather: Louie Henderson, Jr.
Born – Houston, Texas / 1900

Great Grandmother: (Louie Jr.'s Mother) Emma Washington
Born – Hearne or Galveston, Texas / 1882

Great Grandfather: (Louie Jr.'s Father) Louie Henderson, Sr.
Born – Hearne or Galveston, Texas / 1880

Great Grandmother: (Margurite's Mother) Ernestine Cordova
Born – New Orleans, Louisiana / 5-3-1872
(Black; French; Portuguese; Indian; Russian)

Great Grandfather: (Margurite's Father) Anthony Jerome Rixner
Born – New Orleans, Louisiana / 1862
(Black; French; Indian)

Great – Great Grandmother: (Emma's Mother) Edith Johnson
Born – Hearne, Texas / 1854

Great – Great Grandfather: (Emma's Father) Thomas Washington
Born – Hearne, Texas / 1852

Great – Great – Great Grandmother: (Ernestine's Cardova's Mother) Josephine? – Maiden name
Born – New Orleans, Louisiana / 1853
Or Paris, France
(Indian; French; Russian)

Great – Great – Great Grandfather: (Ernestine Cordova's Father) Pedro Cordova
Born – New Orleans, Louisiana / 1847
(Black; Portuguese; Spanish; French)

His father was from Brazil. His mother was from France. Her name was Edithaea.

This is the blood lineage of my mother, Ernestine Edith Henderson Johnson – Mitchell.

Paternal

Father: Travis Johnson II
                                Born – Hearne, Texas / 5-5-15

Grandmother: Sarah Williams
                                Born – Hearne, Texas / 1897
                                (Black; Indian)

Grandfather: Travis Johnson, Sr.
                                Born – Hearne, Texas / 1895
                                (Black; German; Indian)

**Great – Great
Grandmother:**   Julia ? Maiden name
(Travis, Sr.'s   Born – Hearne, Texas
Mother)   (Black; Indian)

**Great – Great
Grandfather:**   John Dulley Collins
(Travis, Sr.'s   Born – Groveton, Texas
Father)   (German)

John Dulley Collins was the biological father of my grandfather Travis Johnson, Sr., who took the name of his stepfather (Johnson).

**Great – Great
Grandmother:**   Elizabeth Thomas
(Sara's Mother)   Born – Hearne, Texas
                                (She was three-quarters Indian)

**Great – Great
Grandfather:**   Tobe Williams
(Sara's Father)   Born – Hearne, Texas / 1876
                                (Black; Indian)

Elizabeth Thomas' mother was full-blood Indian. Her father was half-Indian and half-Black. The Indian Nations in my family, **Choctaw, Cherokee** and **Black Foot**.

Prayers of Inspiration

AL FATIHAH

*In the Name of Allah, the Beneficent, the Merciful
All Praise Is Due to Allah, the Lord of the Worlds,
the Beneficent, the Merciful.
Master of the Day of Requital, Thee Do We Serve
and Thee Do We Beseech for Help.
O' Allah Guide Us on the Right Path,
The Path of Those Upon Whom Thou Hast
Bestowed Thy Favors, and Not the
Path of Those Upon Whom Thy Wrath is Brought
Down, Nor Of Those Who Go Astray.*

Amen.

The Lord's Prayer

*Our Father, Who Art In Heaven,
Hallowed Be Thy Name I Am,
I Am Thy Kingdom Come,
I Am Thy Will Be Done,
I Am On Earth Even As I Am In Heaven,
I Am Giving This Day Daily Bread To All,
I Am Forgiving All Life This Day Even As I Am Also All Life Forgiving
Me,
I Am Leading All Men Away From Temptation,
I Am Delivering All Men From Evil Condition,
I Am The Kingdom
I Am The Power
And I Am The Glory Of God,
Eternal Manifestation, All This I Am.*

Ascended Masters' Teachings as taught by Elizabeth Clare Prophet of Church Universal And Triumphant

"Have Faith in God. Anyone who says to this mountain, arise and hurl thyself into the sea, and does not waiver in his heart, but believes that whatever he says, will be done, it shall be done for him. All things whatever you ask for in prayer, believe that you shall receive and it shall come to you."

Mark 11:22

"Lord, make me an instrument of your peace; where there is hatred, let me sow love; Where there is injury, pardon; Where there is doubt, faith; Where there is despair, hope; Where there is darkness, light; And where there is sadness, joy.

O' Divine Master, grant that I may not so much seek to be consoled as to console; To be understood as to understand; To be loved as to love; For it is in giving that we receive; It is in pardoning that we are pardoned; And it is in dying that we are born to Eternal LIFE."

St. Francis of Assisi

SUCCESS PRAYER

O Allah, we beseech Your Help and ask Your Mercy. For we believe in You and trust in You for all that we need. We are helpers in Your Cause with Your Apostle. Please grant to us success.

Serenity Prayer

Allah (God) grant me the serenity to accept the things I cannot change;
courage to change the things I can;
and wisdom to know the difference.

Living one day at a time; Enjoying one moment at a time;
Accepting hardships as the pathway to peace;
Taking, as He did, this sinful world as it is, not as I would have it;
Trusting that He will make all things right if I surrender to His Will;
That I may be reasonably happy in this life and supremely happy with Him
Forever in the next.
Amen.

References

In my "Memories", I reflect on the many letters I have received from various persons who have attested to my professionalism and have recommended and/ or thanked me for services provided. I treasure the words passed on in writings of kind expressions. The 22 references include: *Who's Who of American Women and the Extension of Remarks by the Honorable John Conyers Jr., Democrat of Michigan, submitted in the Congressional Record during the proceedings and debates of the 93'rd Congress, Second Session.*

God Is Love, For He saved A Wretched Like Me,
And Has Blessed My Comings And Goings!

****

(Footnotes)
[1] Peterson, A. (Winter, 2006). Where Africa also lives. *American Legacy, 66-84*

Much of what was in this article was reminiscent of my own adventures in Brazil.

WHO'S WHO OF AMERICAN WOMEN

Marquis *Who's Who* has published its 24th 2004-2005 edition of *Who's Who of American Women*. It has comprehensive biographical profiles as diverse from Sandra Day O'Conner, the first woman Supreme Court Justice, to Michelle Wie, fourteen years of age golf phenomenon.

The *Who's Who of American Women* presents a wide scope picture on the status of today's American women involved in all areas of enterprise and endeavors, from CEO's, Lawyers, Entrepreneurs, Technologist, Government Officials and key women from almost every known profession.

Out of the 32,000 listings of women within the United States, the Honorable Minister Louis Farrakhan's Chief of Protocol, Sister Claudette Marie Muhammad and Sister Latonya Walker Muhammad a Control Engineer, who is a member of Mosque #1 in Detroit, Michigan, were selected. Their biographical sketch is found on Page 983.

The women who are selected for *Who's Who of American Women* is based on either two factors: (1) the position of responsibility held, or (2) the level of achievement attained by the individual. The objective qualitative criteria is also considered for admission of an individual's achievements. *Who's Who of American Women* selection process is done by its Board of Directors and Editorial Board. Each woman must have attained conspicuous achievement. Final decisions on inclusion or exclusion are done after extensive discussion, evaluation, and deliberation.

All profiles published in *Who's Who of American Women* are available on *Who's Who* on the Web (www.marquisewhoswho.com).

Claudette Marie Muhammad

OFFICE OF THE GOVERNOR
207 State Capitol, Springfield, Illinois 62706

ROD BLAGOJEVICH
GOVERNOR

March 1, 2005

Sister Claudette Marie Johnson
Chief of Protocol
Nation of Islam
5020 South Lake Shore Drive
Suite N3417
Chicago, Illinois 60615

Dear Sister Johnson:

It is my pleasure to invite you to serve as a member of the new, re-constituted Governor's Commission on Discrimination and Hate Crimes.

As you may know, the Governor's Commission on Discrimination and Hates Crimes was originally created to ensure that state and local governments, including law enforcement officials and members of the judicial system, respond swiftly to incidents of discrimination and hate crimes. In order to further the State of Illinois' efforts to combat discrimination and hate-based violence, I will soon issue a new Executive Order re-establishing the Governor's Commission on Discrimination and Hate Crimes. In addition to the commission's original purpose, the re-constituted commission will work with local governments, law enforcement officials, educators, and community organizations by assisting with the development of resources, training, and information that allows for a swift and efficient response to hate motivated crimes and incidents. It will also serve to facilitate collaboration among educators throughout Illinois on issues confronting discrimination, teaching acceptance and embracing diversity at academic institutions.

Enclosed you will find the paperwork that is necessary for your appointment to the commission. Please complete the documentation and return it to my office at your earliest convenience. If you do not wish to participate or have further questions, please contact Jill Hayden, Director of Boards and Commissions, at (217) 782-1145. Your prompt reply is greatly appreciated.

Sincerely,

Rod Blagojevich
Governor

Letter of Invitation from Governor Rod Blagojevich to serve on the Governor's Commission on Discrimination and Hate Crimes

129

CONGRESS OF THE UNITED STATES
HOUSE OF REPRESENTATIVES
WASHINGTON, D.C. 20515

EDDIE BERNICE JOHNSON
THIRTIETH DISTRICT
TEXAS

December 28, 2000

Sister Claudette Marie Muhammad
Chief of Protocol
The Nation of Islam
National Center, Mosque Mayam
7351 South Stoney Island
Chicago, IL 60649

Dear Sister Muhammad:

Thank you for your kind words regarding my recent election to the chairmanship position of the Congressional Black Caucus. Your thoughtfulness is very much appreciated. As the new chair, I am excited about the accomplishments the Caucus will achieve with your help and support.

Once again, please know how much I appreciate your support. May this holiday season and new year bring you and your loved ones much happiness.

Sincerely,

Eddie Bernice Johnson
Member of Congress

EBJ/bjh

Thank You Letter from Congresswoman Eddie Bernice Johnson (D-TX)

Claudette Marie Muhammad

Minister Louis Farrakhan
NATIONAL REPRESENTATIVE OF THE HONORABLE ELIJAH MUHAMMAD
AND
THE NATION OF ISLAM

IN THE NAME OF ALLAH, THE BENEFICENT, THE MERCIFUL.

December 20, 2000

Sister Claudette Marie Muhammad
National Deputy Director M.F.M.
5020 S. LakeShore Dr., N3417
Chicago, IL 60615

As-Salaam Alaikum. (Peace Be Unto You)

Dear Sister Claudette,

May this letter find you in the best of health and spirit.

I am writing this letter to personally thank you for your support of the Million Family March, and, your great effort to make it successful.

It is my hope and prayer that we will continue to work together for political and economic change on behalf of the millions of families who attended the Million Family March and who watched via television and satellite.

I pray that in the year 2001 we will see the benefit of the Victory that Allah (God) gave to us on October 16th.

Again, I thank you from the depth of my heart and I pray that Allah (God) will continue to bless us in our efforts of mobilization for the common good of humanity.

May Allah (God) bless you and your family with Peace and Prosperity in the coming New Year.

I Am Your Brother and Servant,

The Honorable Minister Louis Farrakhan
Servant to the Lost-Found
Nation of Islam in the West

HMLF/sm

4855 South Woodlawn Avenue   CHICAGO, ILLINOIS 60615

Thank You Letter from the Honorable Minister Louis Farrakhan regarding the "Million Family March"

CAROL MOSELEY-BRAUN
ILLINOIS

United States Senate
WASHINGTON, D. C. 20510-1303

November 10, 1998

Sister Claudette Muhammad
The Nation of Islam
7351 S. Stony Island
Chicago, IL 60649

Dear Sister Muhammad:

Thank you so much for your call. My spirit was very much in need of consoling, and your thoughtfulness made the sadness more bearable.

I will always remember your kindness and value your friendship.

Sincerely,

Carol Moseley-Braun
United States Senator

CMB:lms

Thank You Letter from former Senator Carol Moseley-Brown

October 5, 1998

Sister Claudette Marie Muhammad
Chief of Protocol to The Honorable Minister Louis Farrakhan
7351 South Stony Island
Chicago, Illinois 60649

Dear Sister Claudette Marie Muhammad,

It was a pleasure to make your acquaintance and receive Minister Farrakhan's documentary and concert performance.

Thank you for attending World Trade Center Chicago's ("WTCC") reception for the Zimbabwe Trade delegation. The African Trade Institute program will host future delegations from Africa. I hope you will be able to attend.

Sincerely,

Amb. Allan N. Lever
President

Thank You Letter for attendance at World Trade Center Chicago's reception for
The African Trade Institute

THE WHITE HOUSE

WASHINGTON

December 24, 1996

Sister Claudette Marie Muhammad
Chief of Protocol for Louis Farrakhan
The Nation of Islam
7351 South Stony Island
Chicago, IL 60649

Dear Sister Muhammad:

Thank you for the letter you recently faxed me on behalf of Louis Farrakhan and your National Board. Your thoughtful words made the President's announcement of my Secretary of Labor nomination even more memorable.

I am grateful for your support.

With best wishes,

Sincerely,

Alexis M. Herman
Assistant to the President and
Director of Public Liaison

Thank You Letter regarding President Bill Clinton's nomination of Ms. Alexis M. Herman as Secretary of Labor

OFFICE OF THE MAYOR
CITY OF CHICAGO

RICHARD M. DALEY
MAYOR

March 7, 1995

Dear Sister Claudette:

Thank you for your letter and the magazine.

It was a pleasure to receive Ghanaian First Lady Mrs. Agyeman-Rawlings in my office and welcome her to Chicago. I appreciate your thoughtfulness in sending me a copy of the *Jet* magazine highlighting this event.

Sincerely,

Mayor

Sister Claudette Marie Muhammad
Chief of Protocol
The Nation of Islam
7351 South Stony Island
Chicago, Illinois 60649

Thank You Letter from Mayor Richard M. Daley regarding former First Lady of Ghana, Mrs. Agyeman-Rawlings' 1995 visit to Chicago

Bill Clinton

April 19, 1995

Claudette Muhammad
Nation Of Islam
1325 Emerson St. NW Apt. 302
Washington, DC 20011-6931

Dear Claudette Muhammad:

In a few days, I will formally announce my decision to seek reelection as President of the United States.

Before meeting with the press, I wanted to contact you personally to give you the news. And before beginning this new campaign, I want to invite you to become a member of the National Steering Committee for my reelection effort.

Membership on my National Steering Committee is an honorary position. It is my way of saying thank you for your past friendship. And it is my way of asking you to join me in this new campaign.

All members of the committee will receive periodic briefings on the progress of the campaign. You will have an opportunity to provide my campaign team with written input about the political situation in your area. You will also receive a certificate recognizing your membership. But no meetings or formal duties are required.

I have enclosed a reply card for you to indicate whether or not you accept this invitation. Whatever your answer, please respond soon so that I will know your decision and we can finalize our nationwide membership roster.

And as you consider your decision, I hope you will consider how this campaign will shape our future in America.

Today, the Republican leadership in Congress is claiming a public mandate to enact an agenda of radical and dangerous dimensions.

Their Contract with America would cut education funding including school lunches, student loans and our national service program, reduce Medicare benefits and enact welfare reforms so irresponsible

and underfunded that they could literally leave
millions of children destitute and without support.
They would legalize assault weapons, break the
commitment of our crime bill to hire 100,000 police
and end our government's ability to create new
regulations needed to protect the environment and the
health and safety of American workers.

Americans are understandably frustrated and
eager for change. But there are no mandates to
support these short-sighted and dangerous measures.

The 1996 elections will be a referendum on how
we want to live together, work together and prosper
together in America.

Will we continue my efforts to restore the
American Dream, to grow the middle class and shrink
the underclass? Or will America pursue a different
vision which reduces government to an entity without
room for helping children, community responsibility
or sensible regulation to protect ordinary Americans?

You understand the importance of the task ahead.
My message to you is that I need your partnership
once again to succeed in the most challenging
campaign I will ever face.

I deeply appreciate your past friendship and
support and all that you have helped me accomplish.
Please let me know that you will be with me again by
returning the enclosed card right away.

Sincerely,

Bill Clinton

P.S. One of our important challenges is raising
funds for the campaign ahead. Membership on the
National Steering Committee does not require a
contribution of any kind. However, if you can afford
to send a gift to help fund the start-up of our
campaign operation, please do so when you return your
card. I will greatly appreciate any help you can
provide.

Former President Bill Clinton's invitation to serve on his National Steering Committee for his re-election

Minister Louis Farrakhan
NATIONAL REPRESENTATIVE OF THE HONORABLE ELIJAH MUHAMMAD
AND
THE NATION OF ISLAM

IN THE NAME OF ALLAH, THE BENEFICENT, THE MERCIFUL.
I BEAR WITNESS THAT THERE IS NO GOD BUT ALLAH AND
I BEAR WITNESS THAT MUHAMMAD IS HIS MESSENGER.

December 18, 1995

Sister Claudette M. Muhammad
Chief of Protocol/Nation of Islam
5020 South Lake Shore Drive
Chicago, IL 60615

As-Salaam Alaikum.
(Peace Be Unto You)

Dear Sister Claudette ,

May this letter find you and your family in the best of health and spirit.

I know this letter of thanks is late in coming to you. I was so overwhelmed
by the miracle Allah (God) wrought through us that I had to stop, become
quiet, and reflect on this Great Day of Atonement, Reconciliation and
Responsibility to seek Allah's (God's) Guidance as to what the next steps
should be.

I personally want to thank you for all that you said and did to make this
wonderful day what it was. Allah (God) showed us that we can work
together when the cause is more noble and more righteous than that which
keeps us apart from each other.

I shall always be indebted to Allah (God) for this miracle and I shall always
be grateful to Him for touching your heart and allowing you to be so
important to this event which gave each of us a place in history and probably
gave all of us a degree of immortality.

4855 South Woodlawn Avenue   CHICAGO, ILLINOIS 60615

Page 2

May Allah (God) shower upon you and yours His Richest Blessings and I pray that He continues to feed us His Spirit that we may lovingly correct each other that all of us may be made better servants of our people and all of humanity.

As-Salaam Alaikum
I Am Your Brother and Servant,

The Honorable Minister Louis Farrakhan
Servant to the Lost-Found
Nation of Islam in the West

HMLF/sm

Thank You Letter from the Honorable Minister Louis Farrakhan regarding the "Million Man March"

BOBBY L. RUSH
1ST DISTRICT, ILLINOIS

Congress of the United States
House of Representatives
Washington, DC 20515-1301

March 3, 1993

Sis. Claudia Muhammad
Nation of Islam
7357 S. Stony Island Av.
Chicago, IL 60619

Dear Sis. Muhammad:

I would like to thank you for attending the February 19th meeting with Commerce Secretary Ron Brown. Your attendance demonstrated your commitment towards addressing the economic concerns that affect our community.

As the Congress begins to focus on President Clinton's economic plan for the nation, I want to ensure you that revitalizing the economic base within our community is my top priority.

If I can be of assistance to you in the future, please do not hesitate to call.

Sincerely,

Bobby L. Rush
Member of Congress

BR:s

Thank You Letter from Congressman Bobby Rush regarding the late Commerce Secretary, Mr. Ron Brown

MERVYN M. DYMALLY
Thirty-First District
California

Congress of the United States
House of Representatives
Washington, DC 20515

1717 Longworth Building
Washington DC 20515
(202) 225-5425

COMMITTEES
FOREIGN AFFAIRS
POST OFFICE AND CIVIL SERVICE
Chairman, Subcommittee on
Census and Population
DISTRICT OF COLUMBIA
Chairman, Subcommittee on
Judiciary and Education

March 23, 1988

TO WHOM IT MAY CONCERN:

I wish to recommend Ms. Claudette Johnson for a position with
the District of Columbia. I have known Ms. Johnson for several
years, both professionally and personally. She is a competent,
hard-working and very dedicated individual in completing her
assignments.

Ms. Johnson's background consists of experience as secretary
to my former colleague, Representative Lionel Van Deerlin;
Advisor to the Presidential Commission on Civil Disorders;
Director of Community Affairs at the University of the District
of Columbia; Director of the Deputy Mayor for Economic Development ("Call Program"); District of Columbia, and most recently
as Marketing Director for Manara Travel Agency, Inc.

Ms. Johnson has traveled and lived overseas which has provided
an avenue for her development in international affairs. She
is committed to self-improvement and the enhancement of her
contribution to the community and society at large.

I recommend Ms. Johnson, without reservation, fully confident
that her position would reflect creditably on any organization.

Thank you for your consideration in this matter.

Sincerely,

MERVYN M. DYMALLY
Member of Congress

Recommendation Letter from former Congressman Mervyn M. Dymally (D-CA)

141

RONALD V. DELLUMS
8th District, California

Chairman
COMMITTEE ON THE
DISTRICT OF COLUMBIA

ARMED SERVICES COMMITTEE

Chairman
SUBCOMMITTEE ON
MILITARY INSTALLATIONS
AND FACILITIES

Congress of the United States
House of Representatives

March 18, 1988

ANY REPLY TO THIS LETTER
SHOULD BE ADDRESSED
OFFICE CHECKED

CARLOTTIA SCOTT
Administrative Assistant
ROBERT BRAUER
Special Counsel

☐ 2136 Rayburn Building
Washington DC 20515
(202) 225-2661

DONALD R. HOPKINS
District Administrator

☐ 201 13th Street, Suite 101
Oakland, CA 94617
(415) 763-0370

☐ 1720 Oregon Street
Berkeley CA 94703
(415) 548-7387

☐ 3732 Mt Diablo Blvd, Suite 1
Lafayette, CA 94549
(415) 283-8125

To Whom It May Concern:

I enthusiastically write this letter to recommend Ms. Claudette Johnson for a position on your staff.

I have known Ms. Johnson for fifteen years, both professionally and personally. She is a person of strong character, and I can attest to her competence and dedication in the completion of assignments or her pursuit of a goal. Her background consists of experience as secretary to my former colleague, Rep. Lionel Van Deerlin, Advisor to the Presidential Commission on Civil Disorders, Director of Community Affairs at the University of the District of Columbia, Director of the Deputy Mayor for Economic Development "Call Program" (District Government), and most recently as Marketing Director for Manara Travel Agency, Inc.

Ms. Johnson has traveled and lived overseas which has provided an avenue for her development in International Affairs. She is committed to self-improvement and the enhancement of her contribution to the community and society at large.

There is no reservation in my mind as to Ms. Johnson's capacity to fulfill her job assignments. She is a warm, mature and self-motivated individual who is well liked, appreciated and respected by those who come in contact with her. I believe that a person of her caliber and abilities would be an asset to your staff.

I am personally persuaded that Ms. Johnson is a person of unusual drive, energy and personality and I encourage you to give her your serious, positive consideration. Thank you for your consideration.

Sincerely,

Ronald V. Dellums
Member of Congress

Recommendation Letter from former Congressman Ronald V. Dellums (D-CA)

JACK KEMP
31st DISTRICT OF NEW YORK

COMMITTEE:
APPROPRIATIONS
Subcommittee:
FOREIGN OPERATIONS

SELECT COMMITTEE ON
CHILDREN, YOUTH AND FAMILIES

Congress of the United States
House of Representatives
Washington, DC 20515

PLEASE REPLY TO:
☐ WASHINGTON OFFICE
2235 Rayburn House Building
Washington, DC 20515
(202) 225-5265

DISTRICT OFFICE
☐ 1101 FEDERAL BUILDING
111 WEST HURON STREET
BUFFALO, NY 14202
(716) 846-4123

May 18, 1988

Ms. Claudetta M. Johnson
1325 Emerson Street NW
#302
Washington, D.C. 20011

Dear Claudette,

Thanks for writing and letting me know of your interest in securing new employment. After knowing you for 30 years, I am pleased that you have chosen to seek a position commensurate with your many strengths.

Your vast international experience both abroad and, more recently arranging foreign travel for others, should stand you in good stead in achieving your objective of a career-level position in the area of international affairs. Your resume reflects your wide range of interests and abilities. In addition, your job history demonstrates a commitment to local issues and community affairs. From my personal encounters with you, I know that you can handle yourself well in any number of challenging situations.

I am certain that you will show the same level of dedication and professionalism in your next endeavor. I wish you the best of success.

Thanks for staying in touch.

Sincerely,

Jack Kemp
Member of Congress

JK:nas

Recommendation Letter from former Congressman Jack Kemp (R-NY)

143

University of the District of Columbia

Office of the President, MB390B
4200 Connecticut Avenue, N.W.
Washington, D.C. 20008

Telephone (202) 282-7550

October 24, 1988

TO WHOM IT MAY CONCERN:

This is in reference to Ms. Claudette Johnson's application for employment. I have known Ms. Johnson for about twenty years, and was able to observe her work most recently during her temporary employment at the University of the District of Columbia.

Ms. Johnson is a highly skilled professional. She is reliable, thorough in all she undertakes, and creative in outlining new approaches. Because she writes extremely well and is highly articulate, she would be an excellent corporate or institutional spokesperson. Ms. Johnson relates extremely well to a wide range of publics.

Ms. Johnson would be an excellent addition to the staff of any institution. Her dedication and strong work ethic assure a high level of productivity. Ms. Claudette Johnson is recommended for appointment, most highly and without reservation.

Sincerely,

Rafael L. Cortada, Ph.D.
President

Reference Letter from Dr. Rafael L. Cortada, President University of the District of Columbia

144

Claudette Marie Muhammad

JOHN CONYERS, JR.
1ST DISTRICT, MICHIGAN

COMMITTEES:
JUDICIARY

CHAIRMAN
SUBCOMMITTEE ON CRIMINAL
JUSTICE
GOVERNMENT OPERATIONS

Congress of the United States
House of Representatives
Washington, D.C. 20515

WASHINGTON OFFICE:
2313 RAYBURN HOUSE OFFICE BLDG.
WASHINGTON, D.C. 20515
PHONE: 202-225-5126

DETROIT OFFICE:
649 FEDERAL BUILDING
231 W. LAFAYETTE
DETROIT, MICHIGAN 48226
PHONE: 313-226-7022

January 12, 1982

John Hopkins School of
Advanced International Studies
1740 Massachusetts Ave. N.W.
Washington, D.C. 20036

To Whom It May Concern:

I recommend Ms. Claudette Johnson for the graduate degree
program at John Hopkins University.

I have known Ms. Johnson for sixteen years, both professionally
and personally. She is a person of strong character, and
I can attest to her competence and dedication in completion
of an assignment or pursuit of a goal. Her background
consists of experience as secretary to my former colleague,
Rep. Lionel Van Deerlin, Advisor to the Presidential
Commission on Civil Disorders, Director of Community
Programs at the University of the District of Columbia.

At present Ms. Johnson is continuing her education at American
University, where she will receive her undergraduate degree
in August 1982. She is committed to self-improvement and
the enhancement of her contribution to the community and society
at large.

Thank you for your consideration of Ms. Johnson for admission
to your graduate program.

Sincerely,

John Conyers, Jr.
Member of Congress

Recommendation Letter for admittance to Johns Hopkins School of Advanced
International Studies from Congressman John Conyers, Jr. (D-MI)

145

School of International Service

November 23, 1981

Dean George Crowell
Johns Hopkins School of Advanced
     International Studies
1740 Massachusetts Avenue N.W.
Washington, D.C. 20036

Dear George:

    I am writing you on behalf of a student of mine, Ms. Claudette Johnson, who I believe has attached some information about herself to this letter. I have been encouraging Ms. Johnson to be in touch with you in connection with your much advertised program of fellowsip support for black students. I want you to know that Ms. Johnson is an absolutely first-class candidate for such assistance. I have had her in three courses now, and can attest to her remarkable personal qualities, her ability to grow intellectually, and her enormous drive to do something consequential in this world. I'm sure that if you were to interview her, you would see immediately what I mean.

    Needless to say, I have urged Ms. Johnson to go through the process of sorting out and applying to a number of quality institutions, including law schools (these without enthusiasm on my part), but I would like to see her (and you) put SAIS at the top of her list. Of course I will write a proper letter of recommendation when the time comes-- one that spells out in greater detail what strengths Ms. Johnson could bring to the school.

    I trust I get to see you again soon, friend. Keep well.

                    Regards,

                    Nick

                    N. G. Onuf
                    Professor;
                    Visiting Professor
                    Department of Political Science
                    Columbia University

Massachusetts & Nebraska Avenues, N.W., Washington, D.C. 20016   (202) 686-2470

Letter of Reference from Professor N.G. Onuf of American University for admittance to Johns Hopkins School of Advanced International Studies

THE WHITE HOUSE

WASHINGTON

February 3, 1977

To Claudette Johnson

I deeply appreciate your dedicated and
untiring work on the 1977 inauguration.
The inaugural program was a great success, open to all of our citizens. This
would not have been possible without the
unselfish help, cheerful spirit and long
hours freely given by volunteers such
as you.

You have helped to set an example of what
we Americans can accomplish by sharing
our talents and energies with each other.
Many thanks.

Sincerely,

Jimmy Carter

Miss Claudette Johnson
Apartment 302
1325 Emerson Street, N.W.
Washington, D. C. 20011

Former President Carter's Thank You Letter for working with his 1977 Inauguration

January 28, 1977

TO WHOM IT MAY CONCERN:

From the outset it was intended that this Protocol/Diplomatic Office be staffed with a minimum number of persons who had a maximum amount of related expirtise. When Mrs. Claudette Johnson volunteered her services we considered ourselves lucky. Mrs. Johnson is a very intelligent very personable lady. Her professional public relations background (she has her own agency) was just what this office required.

The quality of Mrs. Johnson's performance here was excellent. She is totally qualified to and in fact frequently did man this office alone. As our work load multiplied the need for an additional paid staffer arose. Mrs. Johnson naturally filled that requirement but by then she had accumulated in excess of 100 hours of volunteer work.

The operation of this office, for this inauguration, was an extreme success. That success was do in great part to the excellent cooperation given us by Mrs. Johnson. I recommend her without reservation for any position requiring independent judgment and action.

Sincerely,

Chester C. Carter

Chester C. Carter, Director
Protocol/Diplomatic

Second and I Streets S.W., Washington D.C. 20599, (202) 472-4000

Thank You Letter from the late Chester C. Carter, Director of the Protocol/ Diplomatic Inaugural Committee of President Jimmy Carter-Elect

LIONEL VAN DEERLIN
42d District, California

COMMITTEE ON INTERSTATE
AND FOREIGN COMMERCE

CHAIRMAN, SUBCOMMITTEE ON
COMMUNICATIONS

COMMITTEE ON
HOUSE ADMINISTRATION

Congress of the United States
House of Representatives
Washington, D.C. 20515

1427 Rayburn H.O.B.
Washington, D.C. 2
BUDT F. SEVILLE
Administrative Assistant

DISTRICT OFFICES:
813 K Street, Room
San Diego, California
(714) 231-8121
ROBERT R. RHODE
Field Representative

796 Third Avenue, Room 1
Chula Vista, California
(714) 426-0252

December 7, 1976

Dear Mr. Moore:

I write in support of Claudette Johnson's application for a position on the White House staff.

I have known Miss Johnson for thirteen years, as a valued member of my Washington staff and as a personal friend. I can consequently attest to her competency and dedication.

In addition to her experience in a congressional office, Miss Johnson has distinguished herself as an advisor to the Commission on Civil Disorders, serving as Special Assistant to the Commissioners who produce the Kerner Report. She was also Director of Community Programs for Federal City College before founding C & T International, her own highly successful Public Relations Agency.

I recommend Miss Johnson without reservation, fully confident that her appointment would reflect creditably on the new administration.

Your consideration is deeply appreciated.

Sincerely,

Lionel Van Deerlin
Member of Congress

Mr. Frank Moore, Director
Congressional Liaison
Carter-Mondale Transition Planning Group
P. O. Box 2600
Washington, D. C. 20013

LVD:sd

Letter of Reference from former Congressman Lionel Van Deerlin (D-CA)

(Not printed at Government expense)

Congressional Record

United States of America — PROCEEDINGS AND DEBATES OF THE 93^d CONGRESS, SECOND SESSION

Artist Ernie Barnes: Emphasis on the Positive

REMARKS
OF
HON. JOHN CONYERS, JR.
OF MICHIGAN
IN THE HOUSE OF REPRESENTATIVES
Wednesday, September 25, 1974

Mr. CONYERS. Mr. Speaker, the impression most Americans have of the ghetto is one of an environment breeding only crime, destitution, and hopelessness. While these are indeed realities of ghetto existence, they should be distinguished from the positive human qualities possessed by many of the individuals living there. One man with such a viewpoint—is—California artist Ernie Barnes, whose 35-painting exhibit entitled, "The Beauty of the Ghetto," will be shown at the Museum of African Art, 316 A Street NE., from Thursday, September 26th to Thursday, October 10th, thanks to the tireless efforts of Ms. Claudette Johnson who also assisted Mr. Barnes with his previous Washington Exhibit in 1970. The excellent and unique quality of the present exhibit already has earned him special honors for his humanitarian work from Georgia Gov. Jimmy Carter,

660-130——39328

Atlanta Mayor Maynard Jackson, and State Legislator Julian Bond.

Through his art, Ernie Barnes expresses his belief that the ghetto must not be viewed simply as decaying buildings and city streets. He seems to me to be saying it is also a place where people live; a place he says, that is filled with love, wit, faith, compassion, and strength. It is a place where there is happiness in daily life and where the best qualities in each human being enable most black people to fight the good fight against an environment that could easily overwhelm them. It is a life of good friendships and dreams of better days, depicted in some of his paintings by a young boy playing basketball on a dirt court, or by a man enjoying himself shooting some pool, or by others just standing around "rapping."

I invite my colleagues to join with me in evaluation of Ernie Barnes' work, the work of a man who emerged from the ghetto through excellence in athletics, and now, having achieved distinction in the arts, unselfishly devotes himself to sharing his philosophy of black pride with the youth of our cities so that their futures may be as productive as his own.

Claudette Marie Muhammad

CLAUDETTE JOHNSON
PRESIDENT

C. J. INTERNATIONAL, Inc.

10 May 1984

My Dearest:

Greetings from Israel -- I have been to all the places you have read about
in the Bible -- walked the trail of Jesus when he did his ministry and visited
such High and Holy places -- places one does not go as just a regular tourist.
The Community where I am staying is Dimona, where the Original African Hebrews
are located. There are about 3,000 here, and in Arad and Mitzpe. Their Community
is governed by the Laws of Moses as in the Old Testament. These many Black people
living in harmony, is a sight to see. Ben Ammi Carter is their Spiritual Leader.
They have twelve Princes -- each holding a position similar as U.S. cabinet members,
24 Ministers -- Minister of Education, Minister of Transportation, Minister of
Cultural Affairs, etc. One woman Minister who is their Minister of Education and
a longtime friend of mine. They have 24 Priest, all who give counsel to the
people and counsel couples prior to marriage. A man is allowed to have seven
wives. The wives live in harmony with one another -- all through the love of
their Lord (husband). Babies are born through natural childbirth. The people
are all vegetarians (soul vegetarian food) - delicious (smile). They have their
own school system which is excellent. I have addressed the faculty; the student
body; the Council of Ministers; the Crown Sisterhood (all of the women in the
organization) and next week I will address the School of the Prophets-- their
University of Higher Learning, which has a four year program.

Ambassador Prince Asiel Ben Israel is their Ambassador-at-Large traveling
all over the world speaking on behalf of the Community -- meeting Governors;
Mayors, Social and Religious leaders in the U.S., and traveling to other countries
meeting with the powers that be. I am putting together a package for a group to
travel to Japan through the contacts that I have made there. The U.S. and Israeli
press write many negative articles on the Black Hebrews -- only because never in
the history of America has 3,000 Blacks exodused from the U.S. and have been
successful as they have.

Minister Farrakhan has been here twice, former Congressman Diggs, James
Forman and also various social and religious leaders. I am willing to help them
because I see their plight and know that they believe in a system where our Black
men can be men in leadership. The woman are so beautiful. All wearing long

1325 EMERSON STREET, N.W.
WASHINGTON, D.C. 20011
TELEPHONE: (202) 723-9125

151

garments, very colorful pure fabrics; cottons, wools, silk, etc. Truly beautiful and talented Sisters.

Their music -- they have all kinds of talent -- which the people of Israel love. I went to Tel-Aviv on 7th May, which was their Independence Day (similar to our 4th of July). The musical group from here performed before about 10,000 people. It was great. The people of Israel did not want us to leave. I met a Jewish man (who is the father of one of the members of Kiss - in U.S. - who dates Diana Ross) and he felt that their musical show was the best that he had ever seen.

I could go on and on about the people here, because this is truly the "Kingdom of God" and to see all these people - men - women and children speaking Hebrew; Arabic, French and little English - because they feel English is the slave masters language. As Original Hebrews we came from Jerusalem - speaking the tongues of these languages - (not French) and were dispersed when the Romans invaded Jerusalem under General Titus. We were then Sons and Daughters of Judah; Babylonia; Persia; Greece; Egypt; Ethiopia; and were taken in captivity and dispersed throughout Northeastern, East, West, Central and South Africa -- even to China, Japan, the Philippines and from parts of Africa later sold into slavery to Europe and the Americas. I will send you a book by Brother Ben Ammi called God, the Black Man, and the Truth; a beautiful piece of work with so much truth about us as Black people.

Last year when Barry White, Andrew Crouch and their religious musical crusade came to Israel -- the musical group from the Original Hebrews participated.

I want my loved ones to know why I am in Israel for these two months. When I return to the States, I hope we will have time to get together to discuss my experience.

My trip last year to the Orient was not by accident -- God directed me there so that I could see the relationship between the people of the Orient and we the Blacks. When I spoke to the Chinese; Japanese; and the Philippinos, they told me that they knew they were descendents of Blacks not whites. Now that I am here, I understand it all. Last week I visited Jericho (the city where the walls came tumbling down) in the Old Testament. I saw Black people looking just like me -- some with skin Blacker than mine -- hair curly, some with hair straight like mine. Beautiful people -- all living in the hill-sides, most are sheep hearders -- as was in the days of Jesus the Christ.

I came to know about the Original Black Hebrews, seven years ago through my dear friend and Brother, the late A.B. Tolbert, who was the son of the late President Tolbert of Liberia. He and his father were strong supporters of the Black Hebrews, who left the U.S. in 1965 -- 400 Blacks -- went to Liberia, started a school there, farmed land, and grew in spirit and body, and in 1970 came to Israel about 1,000 Blacks. They also have an extension in Ghana -- with a school of over 1,000 students.

If you are interested in knowing more about the Original African Hebrews, please call Prince Asiel Ben Israel -- tell him that I have recommended that you call and let him know that you want to see the film done recently by the

Page Three

Israel television on the life style of the Hebrews. He will make arrangements to either visit you personally or have someone to contact you to show you the film. It is a terrific film. I had a showing of the film at the actress, Beverly Todd's home, in L.A. two days prior to my leaving. Prince Asiel Ben Israel and his assistant Brother Ahkeazer flew out from Chicago to be with us and discuss the film. I had many of the Black actors and actresses there. Many of whom will come here to participate in the Writer's Conference in September 1984.

Prince Asiel Ben Israel can be reached in Chicago at (312) 488-0166 (home) or 487-0444 or 224-0104 (office). They have a boutique and Soul Food Restaurant in both Chicago and Atlanta, Georgia. You should go by for a visit next time you are in either city.

Well, my time is running out. I must go and see the children perform. I felt a need to write to my loved ones so that you can get a feel for the happiness that I am experiencing here in Israel, and can see the hook-up of my travels and spiritual development these past seven years. God has truly blessed me, as he has you and your families.

We are all Brothers and Sisters under God; Christians, Jew, Hebrews, Muslims, Buddahs, etc., but the bottom line is that we are all "People of Color" who must come together and take our rightful place on Planet Earth -- number one -- Rulers of the Universe.

God Is Truly Love,

Claudette Marie

Sister Claudetta Marie

I Love You!

A letter written in 1984 to my family, friends and supporters attesting to the beautiful and peaceful lifestyle of the Hebrew Israelites, Dimona, Israel